657X

ART DECO NORITAKE & MORE

A Photographic and Historical Record

David Spain

Schiffer Publishing Ltd

4880 Lower Valley Road, Atglen, PA 19310 USA

This book is dedicated,
with love, to my grandchildren,
Clara Louise Spain and Oliver Jeh Spain.

Designed by John P. Cheek
Cover design by Bruce Waters
Type set in Korinna BT

ISBN: 0-7643-2049-1
Printed in China
1 2 3 4

Published by Schiffer Publishing Ltd.
4880 Lower Valley Road
Atglen, PA 19310
Phone: (610) 593-1777; Fax: (610) 593-2002
E-mail: Info@schifferbooks.com

For the largest selection of fine reference books on this and related subjects, please visit our web site at
www.schifferbooks.com
We are always looking for people to write books on new and related subjects. If you have an idea for a book please contact us at the above address.

This book may be purchased from the publisher.
Include $3.95 for shipping.
Please try your bookstore first.
You may write for a free catalog.

In Europe, Schiffer books are distributed by
Bushwood Books
6 Marksbury Ave.
Kew Gardens
Surrey TW9 4JF England
Phone: 44 (0) 20 8392-8585; Fax: 44 (0) 20 8392-9876
E-mail: info@bushwoodbooks.co.uk
Free postage in the U.K., Europe; air mail at cost.

Contents

In Honor of

Noritake Co., Ltd.,

Nagoya, Japan,

on the occasion of their centennial year,

2004

The firm known today as Noritake Co., Ltd., was founded by Baron Ichizaemon Morimura, Mr. Magobei Okura, and several others in January 1904. At that time, underneath the cornerstone of the power plant, was buried a china plate, signed by Baron Ichizaemon Morimura, Mr. Magobei Okura, Mr. Yusakata Murai, and other shareholders. On it, in Japanese, was this (now translated) inscription:

SINCE THE FOUNDATION OF MESSRS. MORIMURA & CO., WE HAVE WORKED
ABOUT TWO DECADES FOR THE IMPROVEMENT OF JAPANESE POTTERY PRODUCTS.
TODAY WE HAVE ESTABLISHED THIS, THE JAPAN CERAMICS CORPORATION.
OUR AIM SHALL BE TO PRODUCE SUCH EARTHENWARE AND PORCELAIN AS WILL
BEAR COMPARISON WITH THE BEST MADE IN THE WORLD, AND TO CONTRIBUTE OUR
SHARE TO THE DEVELOPMENT OF JAPAN'S EXPORT TRADE. BY THE GRACE OF HEAVEN,
WE WILL DO OUR BEST TO ATTAIN THIS,
OUR AIM.

THE 1ST DAY OF JANUARY OF THE
37TH YEAR OF MEIJI (1904).

Baron Ichizaemon Morimura (1839-1919)

Acknowledgments

Although I alone am listed as the author of this book, it has been enhanced greatly because of extraordinary contributions made by many others. Particularly notable among these is Mr. Isamu Kuroda, of Tokyo, Japan. In November 2002, I spent almost a week in Nagoya, Japan—the city the Noritake Company has called home for 100 years. It was Mr. Kuroda who made this possible. I will always be *extremely* grateful to him, not only for this but also for the many courtesies that he, his family and staff extended to me throughout my stay and at other times as well.

While in Nagoya I visited the Noritake Company, met several Company representatives, toured the fascinating Noritake Square (including the Noritake Museum) and took many photographs including some that are shown in Chapter 2 of this book. The person who had the greatest hand in this part of my stay in Nagoya was the incomparable Mr. Keishi "Casey" Suzuki. Ever the perfect host, he made sure that I saw everything and, just as importantly, he answered my many questions patiently and thoroughly. His knowledge of the Noritake Company in particular and the ceramics industry in Japan in general is vast, and his energy seems boundless. I am forever in his debt.

Through Mr. Suzuki, I had the pleasure of meeting and spending some time with Mr. Hideo Kataoka, Mr. Mineo Kameda and Mr. Tsutomu Tatematsu—all of the Noritake Company in Nagoya. Their interest in the history of the Noritake Company has had a profound impact on this book. Specifically, Mr. Kameda was very helpful in answering my many questions and for providing several historical photographs that appear in Chapter 2. He also was instrumental in seeing to it that I would have the Noritake Company's permission to present these photographs and those that show Noritake Company backstamps in my books. I am pleased to acknowledge this permission and authorization from the Noritake Company.

On leaving Nagoya, I traveled to Osaka where my hosts were Mr. Kazuo and Mrs. Makiko Morikawa. The hospitality they extended to me went far beyond anything that I have ever experienced anywhere. Some of the most spectacular Noritake fancyware items shown in this book were on display in their home—pieces they kindly permitted me to photograph. More professional photographs of these items and many others from their astounding collection are shown in Kazuo Morikawa's breathtakingly beautiful book *Masterpieces of Early Noritake* (for details, see *Bibliography*). He also provided some of the photos of "Nippon era" Noritake shown in Chapter 1 of this book. While in Osaka, I visited also with Mr. Kazuhiko Kimura. On this occasion, as in the past, Mr. Kimura was both helpful and amazingly generous. In particular, he made copies for me of various historical materials relating to the Noritake Company including two dozen or so extremely rare photographs of the Noritake Company in its early years. These photographs are the heart and soul of Chapter 2 of this book.

While in Japan, I had the pleasure of meeting and talking with many local collectors of early Noritake. Of those, I particularly want to mention Ms. Tsuneko Wakabayashi, the doyenne of Noritake collectors in Japan, Mr. Yoshihiro Oba, Ms. Nami Kanemaru and Mr. Toshiyasu ("Ted") Yataka. I also met Mr. Ichiro Makita, to whom I express deep appreciation. After showing me a photo of a very rare item in his collection, he later sent the piece itself to Osaka so I could photograph it when I was there. When those photos turned out poorly, he agreed to photograph the piece himself. *And* when his first attempts also failed (the piece *is* a very difficult one to photograph well), he agreed to try again, with fine results. It is, therefore, a special pleasure indeed that his photograph of that item is in this book (see D.260).

In the nearly 25 years I have been collecting Noritake fancyware, I have met dozens of other collectors and happily consider many of them to be among my very best friends. All are active members of the Noritake Collectors' Society and all are at least as passionate as I am about the beautiful porcelains we collect. Here, I want to give very special, much deserved recognition to four of them, beginning with Gary Kaufman and (no relation) Lita Kaufman. They both have helped me greatly and in countless ways, with endless encouragement and unstinting moral support heading the list. For this I am *extremely* grateful. They are among the most knowledgeable Noritake collectors I know but, more importantly, they enjoy sharing that knowledge and willingly do so.

For well over a decade, Gary has provided a steady stream—indeed, a veritable river—of fine photos of items in his *magnificent* collection. I am very grateful also for his friendship. For her part, Lita has unearthed, with Gary's help, some exceedingly important facts about Noritake fancyware through her search of several important but (sadly) quite rare pre-war trade publications, most notably the *Crockery and Glass Journal*, and the *Pottery, Glass and Brass Salesman*. Some of the most interesting materials in Chapter 2 emerged from that research. Lita also and for some time has had a keen interest in searching for potential design sources for the motifs and blanks used by the Noritake Company in the pre-war period. Her contributions to Chapter E of this book are such that, without them, there really wouldn't be one. Lita's enthusiasm, generosity and scholarly outlook have been, for me, a joy and an inspiration.

The other two individuals I wish to acknowledge in this special way are Sayo and Sheldon Harmeling, collectors in the Seattle area to whom my second book was dedicated.

Decades hence, when the history of Noritake collecting in the United States is written, the significance of their role will be unexcelled. Their collection is huge (almost certainly the largest in the world) but their hearts are even bigger. That I happen to live only a few miles away is a blessing whose importance to me simply cannot be exaggerated. As far as this book is concerned, Sheldon and Sayo spent countless hours (pleasant ones they assured me) identifying hundreds of items in their collection that I did not have photographs of in my files or books. Then, throughout many photo sessions, Sheldon and Sayo helped me find the items, clean them if need be and bring them to be photographed. Sheldon then helped me measure all of them. After putting the items back, he devoted many an evening hour to filling out and sorting literally hundreds of photo caption cards. Sayo kept track of where the items in their collection were displayed (her knowledge of these details never ceased to amaze Sheldon and me) and in general cheered us on. I am extremely grateful to them for the many ways this book has been improved by their efforts but, most of all, I cherish their friendship.

Obviously, my debts to Gary, Lita, Sayo and Sheldon are *enormous*. My debts to several others, however, are nearly as great. I begin by acknowledging those (other than people named above) who contributed photographs that appear in this book. In this regard, I am delighted to thank Judi Camero, Michael Conrad, Dana Lutje, Jean Dillard, Margaret Hetzler, Valerie Herts, Nami Kanemaru, Tom Mathis, Karen McGee, Kip Michael, Dick Nelson, Damon Saadieh, Greg Slater, Vicki Snell, Ryan Spain, and Jerry and Sally Stefferud. I also want to thank several collectors who, in recent months, have graciously invited me to stay in their homes while taking photos: Phil and Judi Camero, Lita Kaufman, Dennis and Elizabeth Rouse, Tom and Gerri Seitz, and Vicki Yamamoto and Lori O'Toole. Their hospitality is something I will always remember and treasure.

I have had the pleasure of taking a good portion of the photos that appear in this book. I am, therefore, very grateful to the many Noritake collectors who so willingly invited me into their homes to handle and photograph their beautiful and precious pieces. I can only hope this book will make them glad they agreed to let me disrupt their lives in this way. For help of this kind, I gratefully thank Christel A. Bachert, John and Pauline Bennett, Dr. Dennis and Susan Buonafede, Judi and Phil Camero, Gary and Joanna Goodman, Deirdre Cimiano, Claire and Michael Conrad, Marilyn Derrin, Norm and Lida Derrin, Patricia Engel, Rosemary Farrell, Joane and Bruce Ferguson, Lisa and Gary Gibson, Janet Gilman, Nat Goldstein, Dewaine and Bonnie Glyda, Gerald Iaquinta, Sheldon and Sayo Harmeling, John and Marg Henley, Bob and Bernadette Jackson, Lois and Howard Joseph, Mike and Patricia Kocor, Jackie and Dave Kopp, Laurie Larson, Arlene Markey, Tom and Cille Mathis, Katsu and Emiko Moriguchi, Kazuo and Makiko Morikawa, Dick and Sally Nelson, Laurie O'Toole, Dale and Sandy Payne, Rhonda and the late John Perroncino, Doug and Anita Ray, Scott and Nancee Rogers, Dennis and Elizabeth Rouse, Tom and Gerri Seitz, Jason and Rose Shapiro, Steve and Lydia Shaw, Earl and Roberta Sloboda, Earl Smith and Mark Griffin, Lee Smith, Bob Suslowicz, Tim and Janet Trapani, Bob and Linda Trennert, Dennis and Lori Trishman, Joe and Rhoda Westler, Nancy and Charlie Wilson (sadly, both now gone), Barbara Winfree, Don and Nancy Wright, and Vicki Yamamoto. Also, some collectors and dealers have actually loaned, brought or sent pieces to me to photograph. For such efforts for this book, I am grateful to Judi and Phil Camero, Gerald Iaquinta, Sam Iaquinta, Lita Kaufman, Dick Nelson, Ichirou Makita, Brian and Miki Matsuo, Lila Owes, Mischele Reynolds, Tom and Gerri Seitz, Carol J. Thompson and Tomoaki Takeuchi.

For help and support that took many different forms as I worked on this book, I am pleased also to thank Dennis and Diane Burnickas, Barbara and Deirdre Cimiano, Marilyn Derrin, Carrie and Jerry Domitz, Michael Gendelman, Yumi Goto, Mary Lou Gross, Truman and Brenda Hawes, Yoshie Itani, Diane Kovarik, Sachiko Kuroda, Roy and Judy Lawton, Louisa Gowen Malatos, Andy and Sally Miller, Neil Mitchell and Greg Slater, Pat Murphy, Tomoko Nakashima, Heather Dew Oaksen, Yumiko Ohga, Mike and Connie Owen, Frederick and Connie Scheetz, Werner and Jeanette Schimmelbusch, Bill and Nancy Spain, Norman Spain, Steve and Gunnel Tanimoto, Tim and Janet Trapani, John Webb and Kosuke Yamaguchi. For superb assistance in preparing portions of the manuscript of this book, I am very grateful to Jane Brem. For help cataloging many of my photographs, I thank my daughter Rachel; for help with certain digital photographic tasks, I thank my son Ryan.

Finally, for their vital and unwavering support in general, I humbly thank my wife Jannie and the rest of my immediate family—Andrew, Ryan and Margaret (who produced the grandchildren this book is dedicated to) and Rachel. For me at least, creating a book like this was often quite difficult; putting up with me while I made the effort, however, surely was at least as trying. To them I say with utmost sincerity: without you, I could not have done it.

Chapter 1

Aims and Scope of This Book

Although the themes and materials in this book are completely new, they also extend those in my previous books on Noritake collectibles. The first of those earlier books, *Noritake Collectibles A to Z* (1997), with color photos of about 1000 different items, is still the largest and most comprehensive of the books in the field. The second book, *Collecting Noritake A to Z* (1999), has more of an Art Deco focus and has photographs of over 550 items, none of them having been shown in the first book. The third book, *Noritake Fancyware A to Z* (2002) has photographs of more than 750 pieces not shown in the first two books, yielding a total of over 2300 different items shown in those books. This fourth book, *Art Deco Noritake and More*, adds approximately 1000 new items to that total.

In this book, my basic aim has been to show a large and also representative sample of the fancyware items produced by the Noritake Company, primarily during the period after World War I and prior to World War II. Also, as in my second book, I have given emphasis to items with Art Deco motifs. Another key objective has been to use reasonably high quality photos that are arranged so that users of the book can locate any item of interest *rapidly and easily* and without having to be an expert on the subject. Although the materials shown in this book were made over a period of seven or eight decades beginning in about 1908, by far the vast majority of the items were produced during a much shorter period: 1921-1931. As I have stated elsewhere (Spain 2002, p.7), this chronology is at odds with the widespread tendency to say that these materials were produced between 1921 and 1941. The latter date does mark the closing of the New York office of Morimura Bros. (as the Noritake Company was known in those days) and is, of course, a year of great significance. But as Mr. Keishi Suzuki has convincingly noted (in an article entitled "About Old Noritake"; see *Bibliography* for details), it appears that the Noritake Company had almost completely stopped producing fancy china for export a full ten years prior to that infamous date.

I continue to be amazed by the large and diverse array of high quality porcelains produced by the Noritake Company in such a short time. I have been collecting Noritake for more than twenty years; I have seen and photographed over two dozen truly major collections. In each, there have been at least a few and often many items that I had seen in no other. With the advent of eBay and other Internet auction sites, one does not need to visit a collector to see new items; scores of previously unknown items appear on such sites every year. This is true even if the items one is most interested in are delimited rather sharply by style or time period. There simply is no doubt about it: the Noritake Company produced an amazingly large and impressively high quality line of non-dinnerware export porcelains during this period.

And, don't forget, for most of those years, these items were, or were meant to be, a *sideline*. The bulk of the Company's output was dinnerware. For over 80 years, the Noritake Company's fame has derived from its ability to produce and effectively market moderately priced very high quality porcelain dinnerware sets. In this effort, the Noritake Company has been so successful that even today, most people, no matter where they are in the world, think of dinnerware when they hear the word "Noritake."

Scope

It can usefully be said that there are two kinds of books on collectible fancyware made by the Noritake Company: small ones and big ones. Contrary to what one might expect, however, it is the small books in which one generally will find photos of the *full* range of fancyware collectibles made by the Noritake Company. This feat is achieved by limiting the items shown to just a few of the masterpieces of the Company's pre-1931 output. With but one exception (Donahue 1979), these small books have been published in Japan (a recent, exceptionally beautiful example is *Masterpieces of Early Noritake* by Kazuo Morikawa; see *Bibliography* for details about this and other similar books). This trend in where these books are being published can be traced in part to the fact that, in Japan, collectors of Noritake Company fancyware porcelains usually (but by no means always) have broader interests than do such collectors elsewhere.

The big books on collectible fancyware made by the Noritake Company are, on the other hand, encyclopedic in character. At the same time, however, they are limited (by choice) to the presentation of just one of the two basic kinds of pre-war Noritake collectibles. The book you have in your hands is an example—i.e., it is encyclopedic, with a definite emphasis on fancyware Noritake made after 1921 and especially the Art Deco items made between 1925 and 1931. As noted above, it is the fourth such book that I have produced, one that may be thought of as the newest in a *series* of such books. These four books are linked in various ways. For example, there are numerous references in later books to photos and other materials in earlier books. Also, beginning with the second book, the items shown in the various chapters of Part Two were numbered sequentially starting at the point where the numbers in a chapter of the previous book stopped.

Although these books are similar in scope, each has had a distinct theme (or themes) that are discussed in Chapter 2. In the first book, for example, I presented a brief account of the history of the Noritake Company and discussed trends in the collecting of Noritake, especially in North America. In the second book, the focus was on identifying the characteristic features of Art Deco, in general and as manifested in Noritake fancyware in particular. In the third book, the thematic aim was to address various technical issues commonly raised by collectors and dealers. In this book, as in the first one, there are two focal points: historical themes and Art Deco materials. The historical materials are both textual and visual, with the latter being a set of extremely rare and important historical photographs that became available to me quite recently. It is especially fitting that these materials are presented now because the year this book is due to be published, 2004, marks the 100th anniversary of the founding of the Noritake Company. The Art Deco emphasis reflects both the character of the materials produced by the Noritake Company in the late 1920s and the undeniable fact that vintage items with Art Deco motifs are now, as they have been for many years, *very* popular with collectors.

In North America, but not elsewhere, two widely used terms—"Nippon" and "Noritake"—designate two basic types of collectible fancy Noritake china. These types differ stylistically and chronologically as well as terminologically. The terms derive from certain details in the backstamps that are found on the items of interest to collectors. Prior to 1921, the backstamps on Noritake products exported to the United States did not have the English version of the name of the country of origin ("Japan"). Instead, the backstamp had an anglicized version of the Japanese name ("Nippon"). Also, the product name (somewhat like a brand name) used by the company—i.e., Noritake—seldom if ever appeared in English on the backstamp of pre-1921 materials exported to the United States. Beginning in 1921, however, new American regulations required that all imports to the United States should be labeled with the English word for the country of origin. This is why the word "Japan" is found in the backstamps used by the Noritake Company for products exported to the United States after 1920. At the same time, the English version of the primary product name of the company was also added to the backstamps on items destined for America. It must be emphasized that customs regulations in the UK were different. This is why, at least in part, the backstamps on Noritake porcelains exported to Great Britain and the Commonwealth prior to 1921 *did* use English to indicate the country of origin ("Japan") *and* the product name ("Noritake").

Because the artistic characteristics of pre- and post-1921 collectible Noritake are quite different, these items tend to appeal to different collectors. But it is only a tendency; some collectors, especially in Japan but also in America, have long had an interest in both types. As noted in more detail in my previous books, however, import regulations such as those mentioned above and matters of taste have helped produce two distinct collector groups in America, each with its own specialized viewpoint. As an extension of this, the books published in America on collectible Noritake-made fancyware overwhelmingly are about only one of the two types ("Nippon" or "Noritake").

Glorious Nippon

From a practical standpoint, it is difficult to imagine a single *encyclopedic* book covering the full range of collectible Noritake export fancyware produced from c. 1908 through c. 1931. Such a book, one that solidly covered both "Nippon" and "Noritake," would of necessity be huge. Even so, this does not preclude one from offering readers at least a sampling of the otherwise excluded fancy items—in this case, various "Nippon" materials from c. 1908-1920. Moreover, since this book is being pub-

lished after a century of creative work by the Noritake Company, it seems especially appropriate to show at least some of these earlier pieces. To that end, a small sample of these materials are presented here in photos 1.1 – 1.12. (Those interested in seeing more photos of items like these should consult the series of books by Van Patten listed in the *Bibliography*.)

Nippon era vase (1.1). 10.25"h. Backstamp: Nippon Maple Leaf.

Nippon era ewer (1.2). 8.88"h. Backstamp: Nippon Maple Leaf.

After viewing the photos, it should be easy to understand why the Japanese art historian and critic Hiroshi Unno says, in his essay in *Early Noritake* (p.12): "Many of the first products of the company were clearly influenced by Art Nouveau." This is evident, he continues, from the shapes of the items, "with lines reminiscent of plants, the motifs of trees, leaves and flowers." It also is evident, Unno notes, in the color palette that predominated at the time: "pastel hues of pale yellow, pale green and pink" plus, I would add, a multitude of wonderful brown tones. But note: Mr. Unno does not say that all the fancy line items from this period exhibit Art Nouveau characteristics. The Noritake Company also produced, he reminds us, "Japanese-style pieces and those in ... traditional European styles" for a period that lasted until the end of World War I.

Three Nippon era items (1.3). Jug, *left*, 9.5"h. Backstamp: Nippon Maple Leaf (blue). Vase, *center*, 6.5"h. Backstamp: Nippon Leaf (blue). Vase, *right*, 8.75"h. Backstamp: Nippon M-in-Wreath (blue).

In the period between about 1908 and 1920, Noritake (or "Nippon") fancyware items were expensive compared to what they would be a decade later because (as the photos show) Nippon era items were often large, usually were meticulously decorated, and frequently displayed lavish amounts of gold. As Unno notes (p.12) "Even the design plans and sketches from this period are so carefully and minutely done, they can be considered beautiful artworks in themselves." (For an example from this period, see photo 2.28, on page 21 of this book; for other similar items, most from about 1920-1925, see Chapter S.)

Post 1945 Noritake fancyware

When explaining the scope of my first Noritake book, I noted that I had decided to include post-war Noritake collectibles for a very simple reason. I wanted my books to include examples of all the non-Nippon, non-dinnerware materials collected by people in the United States who call themselves "Noritake collectors." This continues to be one of my goals. Since many people in the United States who refer to themselves as "Noritake collectors" have considerable interest in post-war Noritake items, these materials are included (mostly in Chapters F and V).

Nippon era humidor (1.4). 7.25"h.
Backstamp: Nippon M-in-Wreath.

Two Nippon era plaques (1.6). 10.0"dia. Backstamps: Nippon M-in-Wreath (green).

Three Nippon era items (1.5). Vase, *left*, 9.5"h. Backstamp: Nippon M-in-Wreath (blue). Candlestick, *center*, 8.0"h. Backstamp: Nippon M-in-Wreath (blue). Tankard, *right*, 8.75"h. Backstamp: Nippon Maple Leaf (blue).

Nippon era vase (1.7). 10.0"h. Backstamp: Nippon Maple Leaf.

Organization

This book has two parts. In Part One, I provide some introductory material (the chapter you are reading now), some historical materials (Chapter 2) and information about Noritake backstamps (Chapter 3). Most of the book consists of photographs. These are in Part Two and, as with my previous books, are *organized so users can find things quickly and easily.* In fact, this was and still is one of my two main objectives. From the feedback I have received (and for which I am most grateful), I believe my approach to the organization of the materials in this book does enable users to find things *without frustration or extensive technical knowledge.* Indeed, the organizational system is such that most readers will not need to have the principles behind it spelled out. The key is in the titles of the chapters in Part Two. They express rather completely the components of the organizational system and, happily, are basically self-explanatory.

To find a photo of a particular item in this book one needs to do just three things. *First,* use the Table of Contents to identify the specific chapter where the item of interest should be shown. *Second,* turn to the first page of that chapter and examine the list of the more specific kinds of pieces shown in that chapter. Then, *third,* turn to the page or pages indicated. Since there usually are at most only a few pages for each specific kind of item and often only one, it is likely that within a few seconds any user can find the materials of interest simply by scanning the relevant pages. Importantly, it is not necessary to be an expert in order to make such a search. This is because nearly all of the various types of materials are defined using ordinary English words that are no more technical than "round and without handles," or "with figural elements." The few exceptions are discussed in the opening pages of each chapter and in no instance are the comments arcane or complex. Finally, if all else fails, there is an index. It not only mentions most kinds of items but also lists certain difficult-to-classify items in various ways.

Three Nippon era vases (1.9). Vase, *left,* 6.0"h. vase, *center,* 6.25"h. vase, *right,* 5.63"h. Backstamps (all): Nippon M-in-Wreath (green).

Nippon era vase (1.10). 13.5"h. Backstamp: Nippon M-in-Wreath (green).

Nippon era vase (1.11). 7.38"h. Backstamp: Nippon M-in-Wreath (green).

Three Nippon era vases (1.8). Vase, *left,* 7.5"h. Vase, *center,* 12.18"h. Vase, *right,* 8.5"h. Backstamps (all): Nippon Maple Leaf (blue).

Three Nippon era vases (1.12). Vase, *left,* 10.25"h. Backstamp: Nippon M-in-Wreath (blue). Vase, *center,* 11.5"h. Backstamp: Nippon Maple Leaf (blue). Vase, *right,* 10.25"h. Backstamp: Nippon M-in-Wreath (green).

Chapter 2
Noritake: The First One Hundred Years

A fiftieth anniversary celebration

On a chilly Thursday evening in November, virtually everyone connected with the New York office of Morimura Bros. had gathered in New York at the Hotel Pennsylvania to celebrate the company's fiftieth year in business.[1] In all, 189 people attended the banquet. Many of the men, it was noted as though it were news, were accompanied by their wives or "other fair ones." During the festivities, the head of the New York office, Mr. Yasukata Murai, offered welcoming remarks and then, later in the evening, surprised one and all by presenting his *personal* check to every member of the staff as well as to some long-serving members who had recently retired. Gifts were given to certain more senior staff members, as well.

One recipient was Mr. Charles Kaiser, the Manager and Head of Sales at Morimura Bros. in New York. Mr. Kaiser's role in the company was important in ways that pertain rather directly to what interests today's Noritake collectors. It was he who had the vital task of telling company authorities in Nagoya what colors, shapes and styles would appeal to American customers. In fact, in 1931, after Charles Kaiser and his close associate Cyril Leigh (the head of the Morimura Bros. design studio in New York) made their last trip to Japan (see Photo 2.1), the production of Noritake fancyware all but ceased (Suzuki 2001). At the banquet, Mr. Kaiser was presented with a special silver bowl that Mr. Murai knew he had long admired. Mr. Murai also received a silver bowl and his wife was presented with a silk shawl.

2.1 Charles Kaiser and Cyril Leigh meet with associates, Nagoya, April, 1931.
Pictured, *l* to *r*: Yoshihiko Asano, Samemitsu Hirose (Company President), Tanekazu Kirota, Heiji Ousawa, Takio Sugano, Umezou Yoshimoto, Takuji Outsuka, Charles Kaiser, Gorou Yamazaki, Toranosuke Miyanaga, Cyril W. Leigh, Magosaburou Horiuchi, Takao Shinomura and Kouji Kawase.

There were several speakers that evening, including Mr. E. Jinushi, the General Manager at the time. In his remarks, Mr. Jinushi sketched the history of the company and noted, among other things, that the company had had an "up hill fight" when the business was first established due to a "lack of understanding" between the United States and Japan. If some Noritake collectors feel his comments sound familiar, it probably is because various Noritake Company publications as well as books for collectors have taken note of those less than ideal conditions. Generally these comments appear in discussions of the significance of the Maruki (a.k.a. "Komaru") symbol found in early Noritake backstamps (e.g., see backstamp M.0, as well as 16.0 and its variants in Chapter 3). A typical account occurs in a pamphlet on Noritake backstamps published by the Noritake Company in 1997 (see *Bibliography*). "The [Maruki] design," it states (p.10), "symbolized a mixture of a calligraphy which meant the Difficulty [sic] that was anticipated when we started business with foreigners whose customs and ways of thinking were different from ours, and a pair of spears to break through the difficult situation. The circle meant to settle everything harmoniously." Although struggles were indeed a familiar part of the business experience of the Noritake Company and its various predecessor entities, I suspect the cultural problems that the company faced were not as difficult and protracted as certain technical ones were.

We return to this topic, but first I want to note something that may seem surprising, puzzling or a little confusing (or perhaps all three). That something is this: even though the Noritake Company is celebrating its 100th anniversary in 2004, the fiftieth anniversary banquet I have been describing did not occur in 1954; it was held on Thursday November 11, 1926! How can this be? How could a 50th anniversary party be held more than 75 years before the 100th anniversary party? The answer turns on an interesting feature of the history of the organization we know as "the Noritake Company." That entity emerged from a series of organizational developments that began more than 125 years ago. In short, although the company that celebrated its 50th anniversary in 1926 is, historically, *very* closely connected to the Noritake Company, it is not precisely the same entity that is celebrating its 100th anniversary in 2004. The best way to understand this, I think, is to start at the beginning with the vision and aspirations of the Noritake Company's founder, Baron Ichizaemon Morimura the Sixth (see photo, p.4).

Baron Morimura was both an idealist and a realist. Aspects of his realism will be evident throughout much of what follows. So I begin with a few words about his ideals (I also end this essay by quoting them). It is reported that, in 1852, when he was just 13 years old, Baron Morimura visited a shrine and made a solemn vow to conduct both his business and personal life with complete honesty (Altounian 1998, p.12). His career as a businessman began quite humbly—he had a stall in the night market in Tokyo—but he soon was quite successful in mining, fishing and various government-related trading endeavors. He soon left government trade, however, because of corruption.

As these events were unfolding in his early years in business, Commodore Matthew Perry arrived in Edo Bay (now Tokyo Bay), in June of 1853. He came at the behest of President Millard Fillmore who had asked him to convey to the Shogun the President's proposal for a trade agreement with Japan which, up to then had resisted trade arrangements with most foreign countries. Whether warranted or not (and there is debate about the point), that "visit" is generally cited as the "moment" when Japan "opened itself" to foreign trade. That it was far more than a moment, however, is demonstrated in part by the fact Perry's visit was not all that successful. He returned early in 1854, this time with ten ships (instead of four) that were much more heavily armed. The result was the signing of a treaty and trade agreement in March of that year. According to Fukunaga, this agreement is known as The Treaty of Peace and Amity between the United States and the Empire of Japan (for additional details, see the essay by Ikuo Fukunaga entitled "The Morimura Brothers Connection," in Van Patten 2001; see *Bibliography*).

As is often the case when dramatic change occurs, some are more inclined than others to move in the new direction. Baron Morimura was one of those who quickly saw the positive potential of this mid-19th century development. One influential experience, as Fukunaga tells us, was his business dealings with Eugene Miller Van Reed (1835-1873), an American with a business in the foreigners quarter of Yokohama. In 1859, Fukunaga reports, "He [Baron Morimura] heard from Van Reed about America and the world in general. This information motivated him to think about a business venture overseas" (p.45). He also was influenced by his close involvement with the Shogun's trade delegation. In 1860, this delegation was preparing to go to the United States as part of the trade agreement that had been reached six years earlier. From experiences such as these, Baron Morimura was motivated to start an export business and indeed, by 1876 (well before his 40th year; he was born in 1839), he and his younger brother Toyo had established a Tokyo-based export business called Morimura Gumi. (The Japanese word "Gumi" has several meanings including "group," "organization" or "company.") In early March of 1876, Baron Morimura sent his 23-year-old brother, Toyo, to New York City, via the American ship, the *Oceanic*. He was to start a retail business that would sell Japanese goods sent to America by Morimura Gumi. After a month at sea, Toyo arrived in New York on April 10, 1876. As part of the Baron's plan, Toyo had begun to study English some months prior to the planned departure date. After his arrival in New York, he continued his studies at a business school in Poughkeepsie.

As it happens, Baron Morimura's timing was impeccable, as we shall see soon enough. A few months after Toyo's arrival in New York, he and two business associates each put up $3,000 to establish an office and retail store in Manhattan at 258 Sixth Avenue. His associates were Momotaro Sato and

Tadashichi Date (neither were with Morimura Gumi). They decided to call their business "Hinode Company" (in Japanese, "Hinode" means "sunrise" or "rising sun"). This was in September of 1876. This company was the first one from Japan to trade with the United States after Commodore Perry's arrival in Edo in 1853. Opening Hinode Company in 1876 was superb timing because the Philadelphia Centennial Exhibition was nearing the end of a *very* successful run (it closed in October of that year). As with all such international exhibitions, there were many different kinds of displays meant to appeal to the diverse population that would attend. One of these was the 17,000 square foot exhibit by Japan (Altounian 1998). As Tomoko Nakashima points out (p.159 of her recent and fascinating essay entitled "The Vogue for Things Japanese in the American Aesthetic Movement"; see *Bibliography*), the Japanese display at "The Centennial Exhibition actually became a major inspiration for some of the prominent figures" in the American Aesthetic Movement. A significant example that she mentions is Maria Longworth Nichols, a founder of Rookwood pottery. As Nakashima notes (p.159), it is said that Nichols "decided to devote herself to the art ceramic industry when she saw the Japanese exhibits" at the Exhibition. European ceramics were of interest to the fairgoers also, of course but, as it happens, many of these European items quite noticeably showed the influence of Japanese aesthetics in their design or decoration. So, just as the Hinode Co. was opening its doors, the seeds of what became known as "the Japan Craze" had begun to sprout and, within a few years, would reach full flower. The place of Japanese art and aesthetics in what was fashionable in the United Sates was very significant indeed for at least a decade after the Philadelphia Exhibition (Nakashima 2000). In May of 1877, according to Altounian (1998, p.10), Satsuma ware was on display at Tiffany & Co. An article in the New York *Times* at the time gives a sense of the interest when it states that "The whole side of Fifteenth Street is invaded by the Japs" [sic] (Altounian, p.10). It was, in other words, an ideal time to do precisely what Morimura Gumi was doing: exporting a wide variety of Japanese decorative and functional items to the United States.

Although far more than good timing was involved, the firm that started as Hinode Co. grew rapidly. It also changed rapidly. In 1878, two years after the company was launched, it was reorganized, moved a short distance (to 238 Sixth Avenue) and became Hinode-Morimura Bros. Significantly, a wholesale operation was added, although retail activities continued. After two more years, in 1880, the firm moved again (to 221 Sixth Avenue) and a year later the word "Hinode" was dropped from the firm's name. The company became, simply, "Morimura Bros." By 1882, the retail portion of the business was abandoned in favor of the company's more successful wholesale business. The next year, the firm moved to 540 Broadway, near Spring Street, a key wholesale business area of New York at the time. There were three more moves between 1884 and 1894, all to nearby locations on Broadway. Toyo Morimura remained active in the business until his death in 1896.

Under new leadership, the firm continued to grow. In 1897, Morimura Bros. opened its own design studio under the direction of Mr. Waki Matsutaro. According to Noritake Company sources, he was known to be very adept at designing fancy china. He was aided in this by other Japanese artists, including Toranosuke Miyanaga, Yukio Takema, Tadao Waki and the Englishman Cyril W. Leigh (about whom we will hear a bit more shortly). In 1902, the firm moved to still larger and better-located quarters at 546 and 548 Broadway (please see photo 2.2; I wish to acknowledge and thank Kazuo Morikawa for his role in making this important item available so that I could photograph it). Morimura Bros. remained at this location until 1917, at which time it moved to 53-57 West Twenty-third Street (please see photo 2.3) where the company owned the entire building. The firm remained at this location until December of 1941. The 1917 move, by the way, was also an occasion for another celebratory banquet. Less than ten years later, Morimura Bros. celebrated its 50th anniversary at the banquet described at the outset of this essay. And there was indeed much to celebrate for, from early on in that span of fifty years, Morimura Bros. was a well-known, highly regarded and quite successful company.

When and why the name "Noritake"

So far, in this account of developments up to 1926, the term "Noritake Company" has hardly been used. When, it may well be asked (as I am frequently), was the "Noritake Company" created, and why was the name "Noritake" used? The answer to the "when" part of this question is relatively simple. The business entity now generally known as "Noritake Company Ltd." was established on the first day of January 1904 by Baron Ichizaemon Morimura and several of his Morimura Gumi associates. This new firm did not replace Morimura Bros. In New York, after the Baron's new firm was established, it was (more or less) business as usual for Morimura Bros. We can gain some sense of this from a ceramic advertising piece the company used for that year (please see photo 2.4). At that time, the word "Noritake" was not part of the new company's name. Instead, the firm was known as Nippon Toki Gomei Kaisha—i.e., Japan Ceramics Partnership Company. In 1918, the firm changed so that instead of a private partnership, shares of stock were issued. At that time the company name became Nippon Toki Kabushiki Kaisha ("kabushiki" means "shares" of stock; in a firm name it indicates that shares in the company are traded publicly). Surprisingly, given how important the name is to collectors, the word "Noritake" was not used as part of a company name until 1947 and then only for the New York office in the United States. In 1960, Noritake Co. (California) was established and two years later, in 1962, a corporate entity with the name "Noritake Co., Inc." was established, with branch offices in New York, Chicago and Dallas.

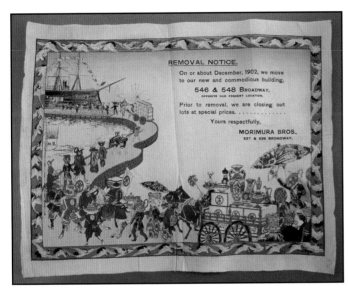

2.2 Paper flyer announcing a move ("removal") to a new location. 12.75"h x 16.63"w.

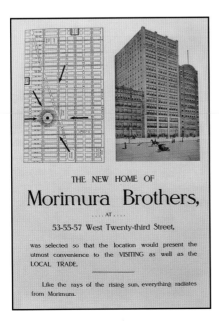

2.3 Display ad on the back cover (p. 250) of the December 1916 issue of *Crockery and Glass Journal* announcing the impending move to the new Morimura Bros. building at 53-57 Broadway (1917-1941).

2.4 Porcelain advertising item. 5.25"h x 4"w.

13

Although "Noritake Co." continues to be the name used everywhere, both in Japan and around the world, there was another name change in 1981. By then, the company as a whole had diversified greatly. Tableware products were still very important but they no longer were the biggest part of the corporation's overall output. Instead, the value of various industrial products (grinding wheels, electronic message boards, gypsum products and so on) had begun to exceed that of dinnerware and other tabletop items (principally flatware and stemware). So, in 1981, it was decided that the company name should be changed to reflect this by dropping the word "Toki" (ceramics). The new (and still) official full name became "Kabushiki Kaisha Noritake Company, Ltd." (The redundancy in the name is recognized but also is seen as inconsequential.) This change of name coincided with the Company's decision to establish three distinct divisions which, today, are (in order of revenue contribution, fiscal 2000): (1) the Industrial Products Group (41%), (2) the Tabletop Group (32%), and (3) the Electronics, Ceramics and Engineering Group (27%). The name that is still used most widely, however, is Noritake Company, Ltd.

Explaining why the word "Noritake" was adopted is also interesting. In 1904, Baron Morimura and his partners began to build their facilities on a large parcel of land they had recently acquired. At that time, the general area was still rural, with rice paddies all around. The short address of this property, back then, was Ohaza Noritake. "Aza" is the Japanese word for what most English-speakers would refer to as a small block or section of a village. In this instance, the prefix "Oh-" or "O-" means "big," so an "Ohaza" is a "big block" of land. Years ago, this word also was commonly used to designate what might be referred to in English as a small village. In 1904, the *full* name and address of the newly formed company (moving from larger to smaller entities, as is customary in Japan) was Aichi-ken, Aichi-gun, Takaba-mura, Ohaza Noritake, aza Mukou, HE510, Nippon Toki Gomei Kaisha. Translating the Japanese administrative and political terms into their approximate English equivalents but putting the address components in the sequence that would be used by a letter-writer from the United States, it becomes: Japanese Ceramics Partnership Company, HE510 Mukou Square, Noritake Village, Takaba Village Area, Aichi County, Aichi Prefecture.

In sum, the Baron's new company, which in 1904 was a partnership (a "Gomei Kaisha"), used the name "Noritake" on its products because they were made at a factory built on land that was part of Ohaza Noritake. That particular *ohaza* had the name "Noritake" because, for some years prior to the end of the feudal Edo period (the whole period was from 1603 to 1867), the area that included it was a large estate controlled by the Noritake family. In 1904, Ohaza Noritake was about one mile from Nagoya which, even then, was a fairly large town. In time, however, Nagoya grew so much that Ohaza Noritake was completely absorbed by it and, as is customary when this happens, the term "Ohaza" was dropped.

Difficulties

Although we now see why the word "Noritake" was used and when the company that used it was established, some other interesting and closely related questions have not yet been answered. For example, why did Baron Morimura and his associates found Nippon Toki Kaisha? (Nippon Toki Kaisha is one of two abbreviated names that were and still are in common use;

the other is simply "Nippon Toki." I use both frequently in this essay.) Why did they buy a substantial parcel of land for a factory? And why did this happen in 1904? A good way to answer these rather important questions is to return to the opening scene of this essay, the celebration of the 50th anniversary of Morimura Bros. At that banquet, you will recall, Mr. Jinushi, the General Manager of Morimura Bros. in New York, spoke about how significant it was that the company had successfully dealt with various difficulties stemming from cultural differences between Japan and the United States. The article in the *Pottery, Glass and Brass Salesman* does not tell us whether Mr. Jinushi mentioned any difficulties other than the cultural ones. My guess is that he did because the difficulties Nippon Toki faced were numerous and the effort required to overcome them was huge. More to the point, however, their achievements in this regard were impressive and definitely worth celebrating.

The non-cultural difficulties were technical in nature. At first, most of them centered on problems encountered in the effort to produce high quality, hard *white* porcelain bodies. For several reasons, these problems did not arise for Morimura Gumi in the early years (prior to about 1894). For one thing (and it is quite important but not known widely enough), Morimura Gumi did not make the ceramic items they exported during that time. They were purchased from various suppliers and then decorated by Morimura Gumi employees. Indeed and according to company sources, at least some of the ceramic items decorated by Morimura Gumi during this period were imported from France! Most of the undecorated stock that the company used, however, was obtained from firms in Japan including several in the vicinity of Nagoya. The largest of these was Harumitsu Kato Pottery. Also, many of the items they exported in the early years were non-ceramic household goods made of all sorts of materials—wood, bamboo, paper and cloth—a practice that continued well into the 20th Century (please see photo 2.5). By as early as 1882, however, it was becoming clear that ceramic items should be and would become the mainstay of the business.

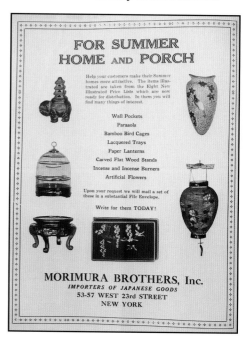

2.5 Display ad, *Crockery and Glass Journal*, April 23, 1925. 11.63"h x 9.0"w.

In the late 19th century, the ceramic items exported by Morimura Gumi tended to be grayish in color and also soft compared to the hard white porcelain bodies that would be used later. The decision to change from soft gray to hard white porcelain was made because, by about 1889, retailers in New York (e.g., B. Altman, and Higgins and Seitter, among others) were telling Morimura Bros. that grayish ceramics no longer could be sold to their customers. They wanted items made of hard, pure white porcelain bodies. Also, at about the same time and for essentially the same market-driven reasons, Morimura Bros. realized that it could no longer succeed if it continued to rely, as it had up to then, on the import and sale of Japanese "fancy" goods. The company leaders saw, instead, that they should shift the company's focus to the production and sale of utility wares—i.e., dinnerware.

As it happens, Baron Morimura had recently returned from a visit to several famous European potteries as well as the Paris Exposition of 1889. On that trip, he learned, no doubt to his dismay, that the potteries of Japan were far behind those of Europe, especially with regard to the mass production of white, hard body porcelain dinnerware. So, for the next five years (1889-1894), Morimura Gumi underwrote the effort to make that type of porcelain in Japan. Although their technical experts, including Asukai Kutaro especially, tried valiantly throughout that five-year period, they did not succeed. So Morimura Gumi turned for advice and assistance to the Rosenfeld Company, a well-known and highly regarded firm specializing in dinner (utility) ware, with plants in various parts of Europe. This led directly, though not immediately, to the successful production of white body porcelain by Morimura Gumi. This occurred in Nagoya in 1902.

This was a *major* accomplishment that required the company to overcome many technical difficulties. This dramatic development had several correspondingly significant implications. The most important of these was that Morimura Gumi could now embark upon the production of dinnerware of the sort that could be sold abroad. This is primarily what led Baron Morimura and his associates, in 1904, to found Nippon Toki Gomei Kaisha (the Japanese Ceramics Partnership Company). To be successful, however, the new company, led by its first president, Kazuchika Okura, would have to make such dinnerware in *very* large quantities. That would require huge quantities of raw materials and other resources (including a large parcel of land near those resources), a large factory and many kilns. Construction was begun as quickly as possible starting in 1904 at Ohaza Noritake (see photo 2.6). Work on the first kiln began in March of that year; it was finished on November 2, 1904. A ceremony for the first lighting of the kiln was held the next day. It was an auspicious day because it was the commemorative birthday of Emperor Meiji. Development of the Ohaza Noritake facilities continued for some years until, in 1912, there were nine coal-fired kilns, each four meters in diameter. By then, the output at Ohaza Noritake was such that Nippon Toki no longer needed to acquire grayish porcelain from other potteries and so in that year (1912) all such purchases ceased (*History of the Materials*, p.3).

2.6 Construction begins on the Nippon Toki Kaisha factory at Nagoya, 1904.

Overcoming the technical difficulties associated with making hard white porcelain bodies was, to put it mildly, *extremely* important in the history of Nippon Toki, but the saga does not end there. Almost as soon as those technical problems had been solved, another difficulty emerged. Due to their large size, the bottoms of eight-inch plates sagged during production and were unusable. Consequently, even though Nippon Toki could make hard white porcelain bodies, it still could not export dinnerware to Western markets because, without dinner plates, the sets were incomplete.

Company technicians responded to this difficulty by working "day and night from almost all angles" for nearly a year in order to solve the problem (*History of the Materials*, p.3). They achieved this goal in July of 1913, again with vital assistance from several European counterparts. Nippon Toki did not produce its first complete 93-piece set, however, until almost a year later, in June of 1914. Moreover, it would be two more years (*Early Noritake*, p.12) before enough high quality sets had been made to warrant exporting them to the United States (please see photo 2.7). Thus and amazingly, a full *25* often-difficult years had elapsed between the year the goal was set (1889) and the year it was achieved (1914). That Baron Ichizaemon Morimura, his associates and their employees kept striving for so many years in order to achieve this goal is both admirable and quite remarkable; it also is a wonderful testament to Baron Morimura's skills as a leader.

2.7 Front cover of the special Holiday issue of *Crockery and Glass Journal* for December 1917 showing, with justifiable pride, that "standard" (i.e., Western) hard white porcelain body dinnerware sets were available from Morimura Bros.

Consolidation and Chikaramachi

Another difficulty faced by Morimura Gumi was logistical. Their decorators—i.e., those associated with companies that had contracts to do work for Morimura Gumi exclusively—were scattered from Tokyo to Kyoto. Prior to 1891, these decorating companies (Sugimura, Shozan, Fujimura, Ishida, Saigo) put their own backstamps on the items they decorated. In these backstamps, there was no indication of the country where the items were made. The McKinley Tariff Act of 1891, however, stipulated that the name of the country of origin needed to be on all imported items. In the face of this requirement, Morimura Bros. created and began to use the "Maple Leaf" backstamp. This backstamp looks just like backstamp ML21.1 shown below in Chapter 3, except that the word "Nippon" appears where the word "Japan" is placed in ML21.1, and the Nippon Maple Leaf backstamp came not in red but green and blue. To reduce costs and work more effectively with those they had exclusive contracts with, Morimura Gumi decided these decorating firms should move to the Nagoya area.

As part of this effort, Morimura Gumi purchased, in 1896, a large parcel of land (12,000 square meters) in Nagoya called Chikara or, more properly, Chikara-machi. The Japanese word "-machi" (and also "-cho") can be translated into English as "town" but, in urban contexts, it tends to be used to designate a named subdivision of a "ward" ("-ku"). It is, thus, the urban equivalent of an *ohaza*. For the next three years, Morimura Gumi moved five porcelain decorating firms to Chikara-machi. By 1903, it was evident that further efforts along these lines were needed, and so a new firm, Kinto Gumi, was created, with the aim being to improve the all-important painting and design efforts. In March of 1905, the firm name was changed from Kinto Gumi to Shinto Gumi but it soon became evident that these efforts to consolidate would not succeed. Apparently, it was too soon to attempt to run such a large operation, so the effort was abandoned. A few years later, in 1909, the decorating factories that had an exclusive contract with Morimura Gumi were again merged, this time as Kinyo Gumi. In 1912, this group became part of Nippon Toki and did much of its work in a newly constructed painting studio at the Nagoya facilities.

Sometime after 1913, a few of these decorators moved back to the Chikaramachi location (the exact time frame for this is not known). In 1935, these decorating companies separated from Nippon Toki and, collectively, became one of Nippon Toki's partner firms. During this period (that is, in the mid to late 1930s), some of the items decorated at Chikaramachi were supplied by Nippon Toki but some came from other, "outside" suppliers. New and distinctive backstamps were thought to be needed for these items for several reasons. First, some of the blanks tended not to be up to Nippon Toki quality standards and/or they sometimes had designs that fell short of those coming from the Morimura Bros. New York design studio. Also, there were concerns about whether US import (customs) regulations would permit the importation of such items if they were called "Noritake." Because the new firm could not use words and symbols found on Noritake backstamps, new backstamps were created with the word "Chikaramachi" (see backstamps C20, C21, C22 and C23 in Chapter 3). The Noritake Company *does* consider porcelains with such backstamps to be Nippon Toki items. The Chikaramachi facilities, which also included a Nippon Toki inspection station used to screen blanks coming from other suppliers, continued to be used until 1942. Today, the land where these buildings were has been transformed into a pleasant public park.

From mud to masterpiece: Nippon Toki production methods

To anyone, it is evident with just a glance that the fancyware items shown in this book (including those in Chapter 1) are complex, delicate and surely would have been difficult to make. That assessment would be true even if the pieces were unique, individual works of art. The mind boggles, however, when one adds to the picture the fact that these largely hand-made items were, in essence, being mass-produced. How this was done, I think, is one of those things that has to be seen, not only to be believed but also to be understood, especially by the layman. Incredibly, photographs are available of the process as it was carried out at Nippon Toki in Nagoya. These photos plus a few pages of text make up a small pamphlet created by Nippon Toki for distribution mostly in the United States (how widely and in exactly what year is not known presently). Fortunately, most of the photos were taken during the 1920s, the very period of greatest interest to those who are most likely to be looking at this book. Production was coordinated by an administrative staff that occupied the main office building on the Nippon Toki grounds at Nagoya. A view of it from the 1920s is shown in photo 2.8. The factory complex as a whole is depicted in a 1920s drawing that offers a "bird's-eye view" (please see photo 2.9). Although administrators were important, thousands of workers were the key to the success of the company. We know a little about the scale of the workforce from a brief article entitled "The Morimura Porcelain Factory" by Rachel Altounian (p.11 of Van Patten 1998). There, and quoting Joseph I. C. Clarke's eyewitness account from 1918, we learn that 2,500 people toiled at the Nagoya plant from 6 A.M. to 6:30 P.M., with time for meals. Although not stated by Clarke, it is a safe bet that these workers had just one day off per week. About half of these workers, Clarke estimates, were women.

2.8 Main Nippon Toki administration building, Nagoya, 1920s.

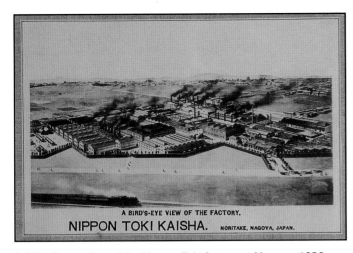
2.9 Bird's eye view of the Nippon Toki factory at Nagoya, 1920s.

2.10 Clay bins at Nippon Toki, Nagoya, 1920s.

To produce a piece of fancyware requires at least a dozen basic steps. First and foremost, the clay from which the items will be made must itself be made; it does not exist in the ground ready to use. Indeed, Nippon Toki technicians spent many years trying to identify the right combination of ingredients. They finally concluded that the best mixture was 54% Amakusa pottery stone, 23% Gairome clay and 23% feldspar (*History of the Materials*, p.3). These earthen materials must be mined and then broken into pieces that can then be pulverized into fine powders. The materials are then mixed with water and the whole is pumped into iron presses that force out the water leaving large disks of potentially usable clay. Before such disks of clay can be worked, they must be kneaded so that all air pockets are removed (please see photos 2.10-2.12). Second, ceramic vessels known as "saggars" must be made (please see photo 2.13). These containers protect the fancyware items from flames during firing. Third, a model of the finished piece is made while keeping in mind that it must be a little bigger than the finished piece because some shrinkage (about 10%) will occur between the start of the process and the end. Fourth, if molds are to be used, they are made using gypsum. If handled appropriately, these molds can be reused many times. If molds are not used, then it is very likely the items (plates and bowls for example) will be shaped by the use of a "jiggering" machine—i.e., a type of potters wheel designed specifically to form clay repeatedly into precisely the right size and shape (please see photo 2.14). Fifth, "slip" or liquid clay is made and is poured into the gypsum molds (please see photo 2.15). When sufficiently dry, the items are removed from the mold and placed in a drying room where they harden. When the items are completely dry, they are inspected for cracks and other defects, most of these being almost invisible to the untrained eye. Sixth, the parts of an item (two halves of a vase, for example, or the feet on a bowl) are assembled and, seventh, the surface is smoothed and the edges as well as any visible mold lines are trimmed.

2.11 Grinding machines (edge runner) at Nippon Toki, Nagoya, 1920s.

2.12 Clay kneading at Nippon Toki, Nagoya, 1920s.

2.13 A section of the Nippon Toki saggar room, Nagoya, 1920s.

After all of this, eighth, the assembled items are ready for their first firing. The items, stacked on small ceramic props, are placed in the top part of the kiln and fired for about 18 hours at no more than 950 degrees Celsius (or 1750 degrees Fahrenheit). This step is known as the "biscuit firing" because when the items are removed from the kiln and cooled, they are as fragile as crackers or biscuits (please see photo 2.16). Ninth, the biscuit ware that has passed further inspections is glazed, usually by dipping the entire piece into containers of liquid glaze. Then, once again, it is placed in a drying room (please see photo 2.17). The tenth step is to prepare the glazed items for a second firing, in the "glost kiln." For this firing which can last as long as 38 hours and reaches temperatures up to about 1360 degrees Celsius (2400 degrees Fahrenheit), the items are placed in the bottom of the kiln. It is in this step that most of the shrinking occurs (up to about 10%) (please see photo 2.18). The next step (#11), begins when the glost-fired items have cooled. The pieces are inspected very carefully and polished as needed; also they are usually graded in terms of quality and sorted (please see photo 2.19). Step number twelve is the decorating of the items (please see photos 2.20 - 2.22). This process can involve several more firings at successively lower temperatures so that previously applied materials will not melt or become distorted (please see photos 2.23 - 2.24). After all of these steps as well as several more inspections, the items are packed for shipment (please see photo 2.25).

2.14 A section of the Nippon Toki jiggering department, Nagoya, 1920s.

2.16 A section of the Nippon Toki biscuit-firing kilns, Nagoya, 1920s.

2.15 A view of the Nippon Toki casting department, Nagoya, 1920s.

2.17 A part of the Nippon Toki glazing department, Nagoya, 1920s.

2.18 A view of the Nippon Toki glost kilns, Nagoya, 1920s.

2.21 Nippon Toki Decorating Department No. II, Nagoya, 1920s.

2.19 A part of the Nippon Toki polishing department, Nagoya, 1920s.

2.22 Nippon Toki Decorating Department No. III, Nagoya, 1920s.

2.20 Nippon Toki Decorating Department No. I, Nagoya, 1920s.

2.23 Nippon Toki decorating kilns (A), Nagoya, 1920s.

2.24 Nippon Toki decorating kilns (B), Nagoya, 1920s.

2.25 Section of the Nippon Toki packing and export department, Nagoya, 1920s.

2.26 A section of the Nippon Toki decorating department, Nagoya, c. 1909.

What and how the decorators painted

Very few of the particular motifs found today on post-1908 *export* Noritake (or Nippon) fancyware items were developed by Nippon Toki artists or porcelain decorators in Nagoya. Instead, they were produced by American, Japanese, and European artists working in the Morimura Bros. offices in New York. In the 1920s, one of the leading figures in the design department was Cyril Leigh, an Englishman about whom not a great deal is known at the moment. In recent years, we have learned that some of the motifs that emerged from the New York design studio apparently were inspired by images on a wide variety of popular products available in North America, Great Britain and Europe—e.g., magazines, playing cards, advertisements, fabrics, architectural details as well as paintings and other artworks covering a wide range of styles. (For more on this, see Chapter E, below.) The matter of source aside, the designs were then sent to Nagoya where they were copied, with great skill and incredible fidelity, by hundreds of artists, both women and men, young and not-so-young (please see photo 2.26).

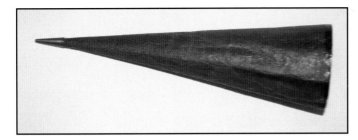

2.27 Moriage decorating tube (recent).

Although transfers (decals) were used frequently (for some, but not all, of the backstamps, for example), I have noted elsewhere (p.15 of *Noritake Fancyware A to Z*) that most of the surfaces of most of the fancyware items were painted in what can reasonably be described with the words "by hand." Even the hundreds of small dots of tinted slip (liquid clay) that we see on so many pre-1925 fancyware items were applied by hand. If you look closely in the lower right corner of photo 2.26, you can see a young man doing just this using a device that is rather similar to a pastry decorating tube (one is shown in photo 2.27). This does not mean, I hasten to add, that all parts of all designs were applied "freehand"—i.e., without guidelines of any kind. Many fancyware designs were applied completely freehand, but I suspect that outlines and guidelines were in frequent use as well.

2.28 Nippon era master Nippon Toki fancyware design, with matching vase.

When I say "by hand," what I mean is that very few Noritake fancyware designs were created by the use of elaborate multi-color transfers alone or even predominately. Close examination of identical items with the same motif suggests that outline transfers and hand painting were used together at times; so were multi-color transfers and hand painting. What portion of the surfaces of pre-war Noritake fancyware items were covered by transfers and what by freehand work has yet to be determined. If ever that ratio is established by good empirical

studies, however, I predict that the result will be that handwork (including the use of aerography or air-brushes, resists and other similar techniques) will predominate and by a considerable margin. In applying the decorations, the artists painted by following a master rendition of the motif. The Noritake Museum has quite a few of these master designs on display as well as numerous examples of two other similar items—salesman sample pages (examples from a private collection are shown below in Chapter S) and copies of the master designs. Of these two special types, the latter items were distinctive in several ways. First, they typically had a measurement scale on one or two edges of the paper and second, several items often were shown on a single sheet. These were used in company meetings when marketing, production and other matters needed to be dealt with. In a few instances at the Museum, both the master design and an example of the finished piece are shown together (see photo 2.28).

2.29 Typical cover for the *Crockery and Glass Journal*, 1920s

As for the technology and chronology of decalcomania (the use of "decals") in the ceramic industry in Japan, I am informed by the Noritake Company that the techniques were acquired from Europe around 1888 or 1889. It is known that in 1890, the Kabe Trading Company of Nagoya, a firm specializing in pigments and other raw materials for the pottery industry, had begun to import decals from Germany. Not long afterward, various potteries in the Nagoya area were making decals using copper plates and hand presses. By the turn of the century, decals were being made locally by lithographic printing methods. Eventually, Nippon Toki was making such decals, especially for use on dinnerware products. Although it could not have anticipated it at the time, the skills developed for working with lithographs would lead directly to the development, in the 1970s, of a line of Noritake electronic message boards—the kind that display words that are read as they appear to float across a screen. As is noted in a Company pamphlet regarding these products, "we were not beginning from scratch. We began with the development of ceramics processing printing technologies and pastes, putting the sophisticated techniques that we developed for use in the decoration of high-quality porcelainware to the production of a wide variety of electronic circuit substrates."

Lusters

Some years ago, I asked a Noritake Company expert about "luster glazes." The first thing I was told is that the commonly used phrase "luster glaze" is imprecise and quite inappropriate. The luster we see on Noritake fancyware from the 1920s initially was a kind of *paint*. Quoting now from a letter I received regarding this, "Luster is a type of paint produced by dissolving a metal or precious metal in a solution." That solution is "a mixture of concentrated hydrochloric acid and concentrated acetic [acid] at a ratio of 3 to 1. Nitrosyl chloride and chlorine are produced in the solution to dissolve [the metals]." These are then "chemically [combined] with balsam sulfide to generate a resin oxide metal compound to which resin is added to give the paint a smooth consistency." Heather Tailor notes, in her book *Lustre for China Painters and Potters* (see Bibliography for details), that "Upon firing, the resin and oil burn out, releasing carbon which acts as the reducing agent. A very thin film of metal is deposited on the glazed surface and fluxed onto the glaze by the bismuth" (p.9). How "thin" is it? you ask. According to Tailor (p.9), it is one-one hundred thousandth of an inch "thick." She too notes that "Lustres contain no glaze and are only as shiny as the glaze over which they are applied. Lustre is at its best on a glossy surface. It owes its beauty to reflected light, so that convex and concave surfaces display different effects" (p.9).

My source at the Noritake Company notes that there are two types of luster paint: those with color and those without. I asked about the colors of lusters used and, in reply, the examples given (the list was not exhaustive) included pearl, maroon, cobalt, iron brown and clear luster paints. The color of a luster paint is determined by the metals used to make it. I was told, for example, that uranium produces a greenish yellow luster paint (or, more precisely, a paint that will yield a greenish yellow color once it has been fired; it is not that color before firing), that manganese produces brown and cobalt yields blue.

I also asked about the "silver" trim found on many fancyware items from the 1920s and learned that the Nippon Toki decorators used two types of "silver" trim paint, one very rarely and the other frequently. The two are silver and platinum. Silver is used rarely because it tarnishes. As for the platinum, there are three types. The first is a compound made of gold and platinum; the resulting color after it is fired tends to have a slightly white tone. The second is gold and palladium; the resulting color tends to have a slightly black tone. The third is a compound consisting of gold, platinum and palladium. For the first two, gold makes up about 70% of the compound; for the third, gold is about 70% and the other two metals are about 15% each.

In the course of this discussion, I also was told how pearl luster surfaces were achieved by the artist. First, the artist dips the brush in the luster paint. Second, the brush tip is repeatedly tapped up and down on the surface that is to be decorated. This produces many small bubbles in the paint. Third, the artist breaks the bubbles by blowing on them. With a dry cloth, fourth, the artist wipes off any luster that may be on any of the painted image that had been applied prior to the first step. Fifth, the object is placed in or near a heat source so that it will dry. Finally, sixth, the object is sent for firing at about 700 degrees Celsius. It is during this firing that the metallic finish characteristic of lusters is produced, a finish that is quite fragile (as Noritake collectors know all too well).

Art Deco Noritake fancyware arrives

Many collectors of Noritake fancyware were first drawn to these items because so many of them were wonderful Art Deco works. Those collectors, and others, will know that one of the most important events in the history of 20th century art was the fabulous and fabulously successful *Exposition Internationale des Arts Décoratifs et Industriels Moderns*. The impact of this exhibit, held in Paris from April through October of 1925, can hardly be exaggerated. The impact was (and, in a sense, still is) huge and worldwide. One of many organizations effected by the design principles brought to the public's attention by this famous event was Nippon Toki, in Nagoya.

The most obvious effect was on the aesthetic character of its fancyware line. Art Deco fancyware items of all sorts were produced by Nippon Toki. What has been unclear is precisely when this began to happen. Given the 1925 date of the Paris Exposition, it might seem that the answer is obvious: it could not have been before the start of the show in April of 1925. Although useful as a "rule of thumb," it needs to be emphasized that the aesthetic features of the items exhibited in Paris were not totally new and without precedent. Rather, their roots can be traced to virtually the beginning of the century and to various widely scattered locations. Indeed, a recent exhibit of Art Deco works at the Victoria and Albert Museum in London indicates that Art Deco begins in 1910. This view is discussed and illustrated in the important new (2003) book *Art Deco 1910-1939*, edited by Charlotte Benton, Tim Benton and Ghislaine Wood. Thus, although the staff at the Morimura Bros. design studio in New York surely would have taken note of the 1925 Exposition, we can also say just as confidently that, from the day the studio opened (sometime prior to 1900), the staff would have been following all sorts of design trends, fads and fashions quite closely. Some of these trends were drawn upon not only by those in the Morimura Bros. design studio but also by those who produced the items exhibited in Paris in 1925. What this means, then, is that we should not be surprised if at least *some* Noritake designs (both shapes and motifs) that collectors today generally think of as being Art Deco were produced *prior to* the 1925 Exposition.

Without good information about when, precisely, particular fancyware items were introduced by Morimura Bros., this would remain only a conjecture. Fortunately, progress is being made in the search for that information. Lita Kaufman and Gary Kaufman, for example, have found an ad in the *Pottery, Glass & Brass Salesman* from December of 1924 that shows a figural lady power box shaped just like the one shown below in D.242; it is, however, decorated more simply. The ad also shows a smoke set with a figural lady cigarette jar shaped just like those shown below in A.254. Whether warranted or not, most collectors would assert that these widely sought-after items *are* Art Deco in character. Because a virtual duplicate of that ad appeared in the *Crockery and Glass Journal* at about the same time and is shown in photo 2.39 of *Noritake Collectibles A to Z* (p.24), you can look at it for yourself and draw your own conclusions. It is worth noting, however, that *the* undisputed expert on Noritake Art Deco porcelains, Howard Kottler, included three such figural items in his famous travelling exhibit of "Art Deco Noritake" porcelains (a powder jar and two cigarette jars, items 2, 4 and 6).

With the tantalizing hints offered by this ad, it is of interest to look at even earlier Morimura Bros. display ads to see if other items with Art Deco touches can be found. The trade journals examined were scattered issues of the *Pottery, Glass and Brass Salesman* and the *Crockery and Glass Journal* (abbreviated hereafter as PGBS and CGJ, respectively). The cover of a typical issue of the CGJ is shown in photo 2.29. A typical display ad from the CGJ was shown above in connection with a discussion of the role of non-ceramic items in the Morimura Bros. export-import business (see photo 2.5). On p.47 of the December 16, 1920 issue of the PGBS, a display ad shows ten fancyware items; none have discernable Art Deco features. This pattern holds for a display ad in the December 14, 1922 PGBS. It shows a compote very much like the one in B.727 and a lidded urn that is the same shape as V.423 (both in this book), plus a dozen other items that are similar stylistically. A year later, in the December 13, 1923 issue of the same journal, the Morimura Bros. display ad features a rather striking basket-weave jam set (like C.200 in *Noritake Fancyware A to Z* and C.276 in this book). Otherwise, the items shown are nice but not particularly attention grabbing from the perspective of Deco collectors today. So far, no Morimura Bros. display ad that I know of shows items that generally would be thought of as within the orbit of "Art Deco" until the one from December 1924 that was described above. Even in February of that all-important watershed year, 1925, a large format CGJ text ad for Morimura Bros. (see photo 2.30) can do no more than lean on that old standby "new" to attract the attention of their customers.

2.30 Text ad for Morimura Bros., *Crockery and Glass Journal*, February 5, 1925.

2.31 Front cover, *Crockery and Glass Journal*, December 17, 1925.

By December of 1925, however, things have changed rather dramatically, as can be seen by looking at photos 2.31 and 2.32. The color cover ad, while dramatic and elegant, is not unprecedented for Morimura Bros. The company sponsored similar cover ads for other editions of the special 240-page holiday number of the CGJ. For example, the color cover of the 1924 special issue discussed above features a beautiful ad for Morimura Bros. and Noritake (see photo 2.39 of *Noritake Collectibles A to Z*, p.23). For our purposes, the image that is of greatest significance is the yellow-toned display ad on the back cover (photo 2.32). Even a casual glance tells us that by this time much has changed. The shapes of many of the items are new. Their decorations are bold and most have motifs and/or shapes that clearly are Art Deco in character. For example, there is a powder jar just like the one shown below in D.241. We also see duplicates of the fabulous figural clown ashtray, the figural lady inkwell, the figural covered box (a.k.a. "Seated Lady") and the wall pocket with figural bird (all are shown in *Noritake Collectibles A to Z*; see A.1, B.178, D.5,R and V.175). We also see the eight-bird vase, parrot double vase, and a thin floral vase—all shown in *Collecting Noritake A to Z* (V.210, V.211, and V.228).

2.32 Back cover, *Crockery and Glass Journal*, December 17, 1925.

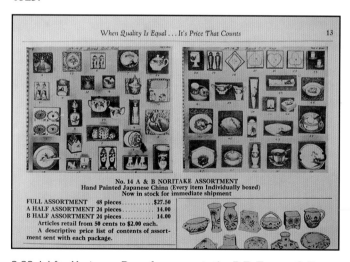

2.33 Ad for Morimura Bros. fancyware in the R.E. Tongue & Bros. Co. Inc. wholesale catalog, Spring, 1931.

As to whether this is the start of a trend, the question clearly is given an affirmative answer by Morimura Bros. itself in a large text ad that appeared in the September 3, 1926 CGJ (Vol. 103 #11). This text ad is important enough to warrant being quoted in full (Italics added).

We are especially proud to announce the opening of the 1926 IMPORT [sic] line from the fact that it *marks a new era in decorated china.* We have *abandoned old styles and old ideas,* replacing them with new and novel effects that will be a revelation to you. Rich Lustre treatments and highly colored decorations, *different than anything we have shown before,* on new and useful shapes, many of them packed in individual fancy cartons to be sold at popular prices.

We urge you to arrange to see this unusual and interesting display as soon as possible and if you cannot come to New York make every effort to see our representative, who will leave shortly for their respective territories with the samples.

In short and from the perspective of Morimura Bros., the basic character of its leading fancy china items clearly has changed. The change was foretold by the items in the exceedingly important display ad from December 17, 1925 (see photo 2.32). It is a change that appears to have been solidified during 1926, the year that, by and large, these items first would have become available to retailers.

A December display ad in the 1926 PGBS continues to show such unprecedented items, including the famous three-piece house smoke set (A.125), the *large* figural lady powder box (just like D.51; shaped like D.238, below), the breathtaking Harlequin flower frog (V.200, L)—all in *Collecting Noritake A to Z.* In addition, a figural center handled plate (just like P.271 in *Noritake Fancyware A to Z*) is shown that features the lady with roses scene (see Chapter E, below, for more on this popular, widely seen motif). Most striking of all, however, we see an actual example of a wonderful figural vase known previously only as it was depicted on a salesman sample page shown in photo 2.36 of *Noritake Collectibles A to Z* (p.23). The next year, December, 1927, the Morimura Bros. display ad shows a Gemini Bowl, a compote with a three-lady figural pedestal, and two vases with a very bold Deco floral motif (one of these vases is shown in V.20 of *Noritake Collectibles A to Z*). To be sure, there are non-Deco items in all these ads, but the trend announced in the text ad quoted above seems firmly established by this time.

It is interesting, then, that the December 1928 Morimura Bros. display ad has very few Art Deco items. Are we to take this as evidence that, by this date, the Art Deco movement was loosing steam? The answer is found in a Morimura Bros. display ad from January of 1930. It is loaded with Art Deco items such as the center-handled serving bowl shown below in B.721, top, and the fine Deco bowl shown in B.35 (to mention but a few examples from this ad). This ad may well be, however, one of the last of its kind because, as was noted above, the production of Noritake fancy china items apparently all but ceased after 1931, due primarily to the effects of worldwide economic collapse.

One indication of the severity of that bleak economic situation can be seen in a display ad that appears in the Spring 1931 issue of the R.E. Tongue and Bros. wholesale catalog (see photo 2.33) issued from Philadelphia, an item discovered by Lita Kaufman. Although rather little is known about the prices of Art Deco-era Noritake fancy china in the 1920s (a Seated Lady with $18 on its vintage price tag is known), it seems highly unlikely that 48 pieces of fancy china of the quality and desirability of those shown in photo 2.33 could have been purchased during the late 1920s for less than $28 (or a bit less than 60 cents each!), even at wholesale rates. All was not grim, however. Catalog pages from the 1930s in Japan show that a wide range of Nippon Toki ceramic items, both fancy and utility wares, both Deco and non-Deco, were being made available to Japanese customers at this time (please see photos 2.34 – 2.35).

2.36 Shinto building construction ceremony, at Nippon Toki, Nagoya, 1933.

2.34 Page from a Nippon Toki ceramics products catalog, Japan, 1930s.

2.35 Page from a Nippon Toki ceramics products catalog, Japan, 1930s.

Two conclusions seem warranted in light of the materials discovered so far and summarized here. First, there are good reasons to suggest that some, shall we say, proto-Art Deco Noritake fancyware items were produced prior to 1925. Second, virtually all of the fully Art Deco fancy china items made in Nagoya by Nippon Toki were produced over a six year span starting toward the end of 1925 (given the December 1925 display ad which surely was produced well in advance of this date) and ending sometime during or shortly after 1931.

From fancy to utility wares, 1931-1941

Business, in the late 1920s, was extremely good, for Nippon Toki and for nearly everyone else. Indeed and according to Noritake Company sources, the Showa Emperor visited the Nagoya factory on November 19th, 1927, at precisely 2:15 P.M., in order "to encourage the people who were involved" with Nippon Toki. Although this visit was not unlike many others made by the Emperor to various businesses and other institutions in Japan, it surely would have been seen by the company as a very significant event. One hint of this is the fact that the visit was commemorated by porcelain items with special backstamps noting the event. Clearly, everything points to this: Nippon Toki was an *outstanding* success story in Japan at that time.

In the early 1930s, therefore, Nippon Toki boldly decided to expand and modernize its Nagoya facilities, in spite of the Great Depression. One component of the project was erecting a more suitable headquarters building. The work for this was under the direction of the Okura Construction Company. A Shinto ceremony marked the start of construction in 1933 (please see photo 2.36). The resulting building was dedicated in 1937. At that event, the Okura Construction Company distributed small booklets with the photos of the Nagoya facilities in the 1930s that are shown here. The main office building has many subtle Art Deco decorative details and is still in use today (please see photos 2.37 - 2.40). An even more important part of the project was equipment modernization. A sense of the change can be seen by comparing the 1930s production facilities shown in photos 2.41-2.42 with those from the 1920s (above, photos 2.10-2.25). Some of the "equipment" that needed to be improved were also buildings, at least in a sense. Specifically, they were the large kilns that were required to fire the tons upon tons of utility (dinnerware) items that were being made by Nippon Toki (5.5 million pieces annually at about this time, according to a sign now on one of these kilns).

2.40 Showroom, Nippon Toki administration building, Nagoya, 1937.

2.37 Main Nippon Toki administration building, Nagoya, 1937.

2.38 Entrance to main Nippon Toki administration building, Nagoya, 1937.

2.41 Applying decals, Nippon Toki, Nagoya, 1930s.

2.39 Boardroom, Nippon Toki administration building, Nagoya, 1937.

2.42 Applying gold edging, Nippon Toki, Nagoya, 1930s.

2.43 Remains of the 1933 Nippon Toki tunnel kiln, Nagoya (recent).

2.45 Application of decals, Noritake, Ltd., Japan (c.1960s).

One of the most dramatic of these modernizing efforts was the construction, in 1933, of a huge tunnel kiln at the Nagoya facility. In such a kiln, items to be fired are placed on flat cars that are pulled along on tracks. The rate at which the cars are pulled and the various temperatures through which they will pass are carefully calibrated so the items on the cars will be fired properly. The Nippon Toki tunnel kiln had six chimneys, each 45 meters tall (about 148 feet). One use this kiln had was the firing of the company's bone china, the first to be developed in Japan, in 1932. By 1979, the kiln was obsolete. The tall stacks had aged, and because they were quite dangerous (due to earthquakes common to the region), they were torn down. Today, only the bases of these giants remain (please see photo 2.43). They are one of the principal sights at "Noritake Square"—the Noritake Company's very interesting park created as part of their centennial celebration. At Noritake Square, one also can see quite a few now empty and boarded up brick buildings from the pre-war era (please see photo 2.44) as well as the Noritake Museum.

2.44 Brick pre-war Nippon Toki factory buildings, Nagoya (recent).

Developments after 1941

The New York offices of Morimura Bros. were summarily closed at the end of 1941, with the result that virtually all of the firm's undoubtedly interesting records (especially from the New York design studio) are now lost forever. During the war, the factory at Nagoya was severely damaged by bombs. This also led to the loss of still more records, including many of the master pages used by Nippon Toki decorators. The work force dropped from a pre-war high of 4,000 to 1,000 (Van Patten 1982, p.14). After the war, however, the Company was asked to begin producing dinnerware again for use by the occupying forces. This development aided the Company's rehabilitation greatly. Even though the military tried valiantly to make sure that the Company had an adequate supply of the necessary raw materials, it was felt, within the Company, that the immediate post-war dinnerware products were not up to pre-war standards. It was decided, as a result, that the name "Noritake" should not be placed on these products. Instead, dinnerware items produced in 1946 and 1947 bore the name "Rose China." Not until 1948 was the word "Noritake" used on its export dinnerware products. As early as 1946, however, the name was used in backstamps found on some fancyware items—e.g. white figurines—destined for the domestic market (see backstamp 67.019 in Chapter 3).

The Company reopened its New York offices again in 1947, at 125 E. 23rd Street, this time as the Noritake Company. In the late 1950s or early 1960s, the Company once again modernized its production facilities, as can be seen from two Noritake Company postcards that appear to be from this period (see photos 2.45 - 2.46). Importantly, it began to diversify its product line by the introduction of flatware in 1956, grinding wheels in 1960, crystal glassware and melamine in 1961, coated abrasives in 1963, electronic components in 1969, earthenware in 1971 and clay sewer pipes in 1972. In the 1970s, a good portion of the Company production activities were moved out of Japan—to Sri Lanka in 1972, the Philippines in 1974, and Ireland in 1975. In addition, Noritake sales companies were established in new areas—Guam in 1974, Germany in 1987, Hong Kong in 1991, Singapore in 1992, and Thailand in 1996. In short, over the past 50 years, the company that began in 1904 in a rice farming area known as "Noritake" had transformed itself into a genuinely global enterprise. In Nagoya, today, very large, complex figurines and other beautiful fancyware items are still being made, but in small quantities compared to the scene there 80 years ago (see photos 2.47-2.49).

2.46 Shaping of tea cups, Noritake, Ltd., Japan (c. 1960s).

2.47 A very large (c. 20"h) contemporary Noritake porcelain sculptural piece on display in a retail store in Nagoya.

2.48 Hand painting a Noritake fancyware plaque, Nagoya (recent).

What the next 100 years hold, of course, can only be guessed. If the future of the Noritake Company is anything like its past, however, we can be sure that it will face difficulties with energy, determination and creativity. We surely may be optimistic about the future of the company, moreover, if it continues to rely upon the six business precepts of its founder, Baron Morimura (as reported in his obituary in the *Pottery, Glass and Brass Salesman*, 18 September 1919, p.11).

2.49 Applying gold details to a Noritake fancyware vase, Nagoya (recent).

No. 1 – This business [Nippon Toki] is established in the belief that international trade is the key to international peace and should make for happiness, individual liberty and harmonious cooperation among the brotherhood of mankind.

No. 2 – Our aim is to achieve progress for the future generations by serving with a spirit of sacrifice and avoiding purely selfish motives.

No. 3 – Be true and sincere. Do not break a promise.

No. 4 – Do not lie. Be not self-conceited. Do not get angry. Beware of luxury, laziness and selfishness.

No. 5 – Do not degrade yourself. Friendship, good understanding and hearty cooperation between friends are greater ties than kinship. They are supreme in life.

No. 6 – Believe in the Law of God. God controls the universe for the benefit of human souls and never rests.

Follow these rules with iron conviction, energy and zeal, and heaven will answer our devotion.

Endnote

1. My account of this gala event is drawn from an article about it in an old issue of the *Pottery, Glass and Brass Salesman*, a trade magazine that ceased publication many years ago (see *Bibliography* for details). I am very grateful to Lita Kaufman and Gary Kaufman for providing me with a copy of it as well as other related materials that I draw upon in this essay. Other published materials were consulted also; these are noted within the essay and listed in the *Bibliography*. For patiently answering my many questions about various historical matters and supplying me with many of the photos and other materials shown in this chapter, I am indebted to Keishi Suzuki and Mineo Kameda, of the Noritake Company, and to Kazuo Morikawa and Kazuhiko Kimura, two longtime students of the history of the Noritake Company..

Chapter 3

Noritake Backstamps: An Overview and Update

There are three topics in this chapter. Each is presented briefly and in *non*-technical language. The first two provide an overview of how and why the backstamps are numbered the way they are. If you are already familiar with the backstamp numbering system used in my books (or if you don't care about this), you can skip to the third topic, a brief discussion of an interesting newly discovered Noritake backstamp from the pre-war period. This starts on at the bottom right of this page. If, after reading this chapter, you want more details about any of these matters, write to me at Schiffer Publishing or consult the third chapters of *Noritake Collectibles A to Z*, *Collecting Noritake A to Z* and *Noritake Fancyware A to Z*.

Defining a backstamp

Not everything printed on the bottom of (or any other out-of-the-way place on) Noritake fancyware collectibles is necessarily part of the backstamp per se. For example, on some Noritake pieces, there may be words, numbers or symbols near a generally recognized backstamp which give information such as the number of pieces made, the occasions for which the pieces were made or for whom they were made. In this book, such words and marks generally are not taken into account when classifying or assigning a backstamp number. Frequently, however, those words and numbers are provided in the captions.

The backstamp numbering system

The rationale for the backstamp numbering system used in this book (as well as my previous ones) is explained in considerable detail in *Noritake Collectibles A to Z*. Developing it was an interesting exercise (at least I thought so) and involved many rules. Fortunately, there is no need for the typical user of this book to have these at their fingertips. Rather and since it is easier, the backstamp numbers can be thought of as being arbitrary, even though they are *not*. How they are not arbitrary is spelled out in Chapter 3 of the source just mentioned. Typical users of this book *will* be glad they know the following four simple things about the backstamp numbers, however.

First, backstamp numbers always have a decimal point and, *typically* take this form (expressed abstractly, here): ##.#. The decimal point is significant for reasons spelled out in the next paragraph. *Second*, some backstamps are designated with letters only and a few consist of letters *and* numerals. Expressed abstractly again, with "L" meaning "a letter," these backstamps typically would take these forms: LLL#, or LL##.# or, on occasion, or ##.#L. *Third*, in general (there definitely are exceptions), as the numerals to the *left* of the decimal get larger the closer to the present the items they are on were made.

Fourth, the numerals to the *right* of the decimal indicate the *color* or colors of the backstamp. Information about the colors in a backstamp is provided because this has been of interest to Noritake fancyware collectors for many years (for reasons that need not be addressed here). In my opinion, the colors of Noritake backstamps are far less significant than many people seem to think. But, because the numbering system I use makes it easy to indicate the colors, this information is given. The list below shows which colors are designated by the numerals to the right of the decimal in a backstamp number.

- .0 = green
- .1 = red (or maroon)
- .2 = blue
- .3 = magenta (similar to but not the same as red or maroon)
- .4 = teal (similar to but not the same as blue)
- .5 = black
- .6 = yellow (including mustard and similar shades but not gold)
- .7 = gold
- .8 = silver (including metallic—e.g., backstamps embossed in metal)
- .9 = tan, brown, beige and other similar shades.

There are two other features of the color designation system that should be mentioned. First, if there are two or more colors in a single backstamp, each color is indicated by a numeral to the right of the decimal. Second, the *order* of the numerals to the right of the decimal has no meaning. A sequence like 15 conveys the same information as 51. For the sake of simplicity and standardization, however, the color-designating numerals to the right of the decimal are listed in numerical order from lowest to highest moving from left to right. For most readers this system is *easy* to master because the backstamps on the *vast* majority of the items shown in this book are either green (.0) or red (.1).

Some Recent Additions to the Backstamp List

Before commenting on an interesting new backstamp, I must remind readers that the Noritake Company has changed the name of an important component of several frequently seen backstamps (in this book, backstamp number 16 and its modern variants such as number 50). That component consists of a circle that encloses a six-armed element. For years, both orally and in various publications (including some of mine), collectors have referred to this as a "Komaru." Accordingly, backstamps with this feature were called Komaru backstamps. The Noritake Company no longer uses the term "Komaru"; instead, the term used now is "Maruki." Given that change, it is only logical to replace the term "Komaru backstamp" with "Maruki backstamp." That is what I did in my previous book and continue to do in this one.

As it happens, the newly discovered backstamp that I want to discuss is a Maruki type. Designated as backstamp A16.1, it is, I believe, one of the older Maruki marks. I am very grateful to Michael Conrad for initially bringing it to my attention, and also for providing the photo of it (see page 34). Recently, when I took a good look at it, I knew immediately that I had an interesting problem on my hands. I also knew it surely was a number 16 type Maruki backstamp in the distinctive Noritake red. So where is the problem? Since red is designated by the numeral 1 to the right of the decimal, one might think I should simply call it backstamp 16.1, but that is where the problem emerges. There already is a backstamp with that number and, more importantly, it differs considerably from the new backstamp (I say how below). One solution would be to pick another number for the backstamp—preferably one as near to 16 as possible. For reasons not worth recording here, I decided to see if there was another solution.

I did find one but, to explain it, I need to say a few things about my early efforts (in 1995) to produce a good backstamp numbering system. For reasons I will not go into here, I had decided that the basic Maruki backstamp had to be number 16. As I worked with the various Maruki backstamps, I noticed that one of them had rather distinctive features. I thought about giving it a separate number (such as 15 or 17) but I also noticed that it was known in only one color (teal). Also, that color apparently was not used on any of the other Maruki backstamps. Given this, I decided I could include it as a version of backstamp number 16 without losing sight of its other distinctive features. I called it backstamp 16.4 (teal is the color designated by the number 4 when it appears to the right of the decimal).

Last August when I was giving the "new" backstamp a close look, the folly of my decision became all too apparent. I could see that, without a doubt, *the new backstamp was a red version of the backstamp that I had decided, long ago, to call 16.4!* Backstamp 16.4 has half-a-dozen fairly distinctive features. For example, the shape of the letter "r" in the word "Noritake" in backstamp 16.4 is quite different from what we see in backstamp 16.0; in 16.4, the letter "r" has a flat top. Also, the shape of the six-armed feature in the center of the circle in backstamp 16.4 is more angular, has more pronounced points at the end of two of the arms and the line making the circle is thicker than in the 16.0 backstamp. There also are differences in the shape and placement of the accent over the letter "e" in Noritake and in the dot over the letter "i" (it is bigger in backstamp 16.4 than in 16.0). Backstamp A16.1 has *all* of these distinctive features.

Happily, the backstamp "numbering" system I developed does not rule out the use of non-numerical symbols. In my 2002 book, for example, I added backstamps from the 1920s even though no numbers in the 20s were available. I did it by using letters along with the numbers (e.g., backstamp C20.1, C21.0, etc.). And that is what I did with the new Maruki backstamp; as noted above, it is A16.1. I used the letter A as an aid to memory, just as I did when selecting the letter C for backstamps C20.1, C21.0, etc. In that instance, the C reminds those who have some experience with this system that the backstamps so designated are **C**hikaramachi backstamps. In the case of the new Maruki backstamp, the letter "A" can be thought of as designating an "alternate" 16.1 backstamp. And, if my suspicion is correct and the 16.4 and A16.1 backstamps

are older than the 16.0 backstamp, we can think of the letter A as designating a more "ancient" form of the number 16 backstamp, too.

There are other new backstamps shown in this book. Indeed, of the 115 backstamps shown in the photos at the end of this chapter, 33 have not been shown previously in my books. With so many new backstamps, most readers should be relieved to know that I comment on only one of them here (the one discussed above). There is no need to discuss the others because relevant details about them are provided in Table 3.1. It also should be of some comfort to readers to know that the vast majority of the fancyware Noritake items collectors and dealers are likely to see are marked with one or another of just three basic backstamp types (numbers 16, 19 and 27). There are, it should be noted, *many* other Noritake backstamps that are not shown here. Line drawings of several hundred (mostly non-dinnerware) backstamps are presented in a pamphlet on the subject published by the Noritake Company (see *Bibliography* for details). Fortunately, the backstamps not shown in my Noritake books are very rarely seen on items of the sort emphasized in them. Moreover and just as fortunately, nearly all of these "missing backstamps" have the word "Noritake" in them, so anyone who encounters one can confidently know that they truly are Noritake backstamps (a common concern among both collectors and dealers).

Regarding Table 3.1

Table 3.1 displays, as succinctly as possible, important information about the backstamps commonly seen on the porcelains that are the subject of this book. This table is not, however, a complete compendium of Noritake Company backstamps. With a few exceptions, the backstamps described in Table 3.1 appear on an item shown in this or my previous Noritake books. This version of Table 3.1, by the way, is simpler than the ones in my previous books. Instead of eight columns, there are just four.

Column 1, (DHS #s), is primarily a list of the numerals and/or letters to the *left* of the decimal that designate the "specific kinds" of Noritake backstamp relevant to this book. Sometimes, in Column 1, the numerals to the *right* of the decimal are given; these indicate the color or colors of a backstamp (as discussed above). In the photo captions in Part Two, the backstamps on the items shown are referred to by these numbers. Column 2 (Defining Features…) provides a brief verbal description of the defining features of the backstamps. This is a simplified guide only. Users should also consult the photos that follow this table. When appropriate, certain features which one may notice but which are *not* "defining features" will be mentioned in this column also.

The information in Column 3 (Year) is drawn from Noritake Company sources, including their pamphlet on backstamps (see *Bibliography*). Generally, **the figures in Column 3 indicate the year a backstamp was _registered_**. I emphasize this because many people erroneously believe that the year an item was made can be determined by looking at the information in this column. For several reasons, this most assuredly is **_not_** correct. First, some backstamps were not used until a few years *after* the registration year. Second, most Noritake backstamps were used for at least several years and some were used for several decades. For these reasons, **the** *years given in Column 3 __cannot__ be used to determine the exact year that an item was made.* This is particularly important for number 27 type backstamps because they are so frequently seen. That backstamp type was *registered in 1918* but *only after September 1st, 1921 did it have to be used.* In summary, the most that one can say from backstamps about the age of a piece is that *it could not have been made prior to* the year given in Column 3. Column 4 (D/E) indicates, again using information from the Noritake Company, whether a backstamp was used on goods *exported* (E) from Japan or sold *domestically* (D)—i.e., within Japan. A question mark in either Column 3 or 4 indicates that the information given, while plausible, must be considered provisional.

Table 3.1: Noritake Backstamps Relevant to Collectible Fancyware Items of the Sort Shown in This Book (Permission and authorization of the Noritake Company to publish these photographs of Noritake backstamps is herewith gratefully acknowledged; reproduction of these backstamps without the Noritake Company's consent is prohibited.)

1 DHS #s	2 Defining Features Of Certain Noritake Backstamps	3 Year	4 D/E
M.	the Maruki symbol alone; usually found on small items in sets with backstamps such as 58.0 and others similar to it; also used on some items for the domestic market starting in about 1951	1935?	D+E
J.	the word "Japan," in colors and general appearance as found on backstamp 27; shown here in green, red, blue, and black (the latter only on some small Chikaramachi items during pre-war years).	1918?	E
J.0w (30040)	the word "Japan," *plus* Chinese/Japanese characters and a design number (in this case 30040); this backstamp is found on small items in sets with a Chikaramachi backstamp; see C22.	1918?	E
JDP.	the words "J. Design Pat. Applied For"; typically found on small items in sets with backstamp 14.	1918?	E
MIJ.	the words "Made in Japan"; found on small items in sets with a #27 backstamp with the style of the letters like those seen in that backstamp but varying in size; in green, red and two very distinct blue versions (see photos of MIJ.2)	1918?	E
MIJ.1w	the words "Made in Japan" in red *plus* Chinese/ Japanese haracters (indicates item was originally part of a set with backstamp 29.1)	1918?	E
06.	the RC stands for "Royal Crockery" and the lines represent a child's balancing toy to symbolize the Noritake Company's intention of engaging in business with balanced management	1908	D+E
07.	RC + Balance symbol + Noritake + Nippon Toki Kaisha + Chinese/Japanese characters; usually in green and sometimes with a design number (e.g., 46755)	1912	D
07.3	same as 07. but in magenta (found on especially fine, highly decorated sets, often with extensive gold)	1912	D
07.7	same as 07. but in gold	1912	D
13.	Japan + Cherry Blossom symbol but *without* leaves and with a letter M in the center; green and red versions are known	1916	E
14.	Maruki symbol + Noritake + Made in Japan + J. Design Patent Applied For; sometimes with a design number (e.g., 39539)	?	E
15.1	Maruki symbol + Noritake + Made in Japan + Chinese/Japanese characters, all in red; compare to next backstamp	1908?	E
15.01	Maruki symbol + Noritake + Made in Japan (in green) + Chinese/Japanese characters (in red), whether or not there is a design number which, in captions, is given within parentheses with backstamp number —e.g., 15.01 (44046)	1908?	E
16.	Maruki symbol + Noritake + Made in Japan (but no Chinese/Japanese characters); green, red, magenta and gold versions are known; see also 16.4, A16.1, 51 and 52.	1908 & 1949	E
A16.1	Noritake + Maruki symbol + Made in Japan, in red; has an accent on the "e" in Noritake, a flat-topped letter "r"and the six-armed central element is thicker than in other #16 backstamps	1908	E
16.4	Noritake + Maruki symbol + Made in Japan in teal; has an accent on the "e" in Noritake, a flat-topped letter "r" and the six-armed central element is thicker than in other #16 backstamps	1908	E
16.4w (25920)	Noritake + Maruki symbol + Made in Japan in teal + Chinese/ Japanese characters and a design number (given within parentheses); has an accent on the "e" in Noritake, a flat-topped letter "r" and the six-armed central element is thicker than in other #16 backstamps	1908?	E
18.	large letter M inside a thin, 5-lobed "cherry blossom" + Made in Japan + the word "Noritake"	1925	E
19.	5-lobed "cherry blossom" with a center of radiating lines + Made in Japan (or just Japan; see photos) but without the word "Noritake"; found in green, red and blue; decorated by subcontractors	1924	E
21.	large letter M inside an abstract wreath + Japan; sometimes referred to as the "wrought iron" M-in-Wreath; so far only a green version is known	1935	E
C20.	the words "Chikaramachi" and "Handpainted" in curved lines above and "Made in Japan" in a curved line below a wreath with a small crown inside; so far only a red version is known	1928	E
C21.	the words "Chikaramachi" (but *not* "Handpainted") in a curved line above and "Made in Japan" in a straight line below a wreath with a large crown inside, green and black versions known	1928	E

Code	Description	Year	Rarity
C22.0 (30040)	same as C21. *plus* Chinese/Japanese characters and a design number, in green (design numbers will be shown after the backstamp number as in this example)	1928?	E
C23.	the word "Chikaramachi" in script above and "Made in Japan" in block letters below a samurai helmet; tends to be on items exported to Great Britain; red and black versions known	1928	E
MC25.	the letters "MC," *without* the words "Made in Japan," under a single feathery branch; for items exported to Indonesia and India	1935	E
RC25.	the letters "RC," *without* the words "Made in Japan," under a single feathery branch; for items exported to India	1926?	E
RC26.	the letters "RC," plus the words "Made in Japan," under a single feathery branch; for items exported to India; green and blue versions known	1926	E
ML21.	a maple leaf plus the word "Japan" in block letters and "Hand painted" in script; a variant of the famous "Nippon" Maple Leaf backstamp from 1891	1921	E
24.	Noritake + M-in-Wreath + Japan (no "Handpainted" or "Made in"); although both are known, the red version is far more common than green	1918	E
25.	Noritake + M-in-Wreath + Handpainted + Japan (no "Made in"); although both are known, the red version is far more common than green	1918	E
26.	Noritake + M-in-Wreath + Made in Japan (no "Handpainted"); both green and red versions are known	1918	E
26.8	a version of #26 but in silver (embossed in metal)	1918	E
27.0	Noritake + M-in-Wreath + Handpainted + Made in Japan in green; the most commonly seen *type* of backstamp on Noritake export fancyware from the 1920s	1918	E
27.1	same as 27.0 but in red (decorated by Noritake Company subcontractors)	1918	E
27.2	same as 27.0 but in blue (mostly on items for children)	1918	E
27.3	same as 27.0 but in magenta (on extra fine items, often with extensive gold)	1918	E
28.	Noritake + M-in-Wreath + Made in Japan + Japanese Design Patent Applied For; ignores variations due to abbreviations or whether the words "Handpainted" or "Made in" are used or to the presence of various pattern names, which, in captions, are added in parentheses after the backstamp number—e.g., 28.1 (Roseara)	1918	E
29.	Noritake + M-in-Wreath + Made in Japan + any Chinese/Japanese characters; ignores variations due to whether it says "Handpainted" or "Made in" or to the particulars of pattern numbers which, in captions, are added in parentheses after the backstamp number—e.g., 29.0 (25920); green, red and gold versions are known	1918	E
31.	floral wreath in "vases?" with the letter "M" at the top and the words "Noritake China Japan" in the center	1931	E
32.	floral wreath in "vases?" with the Maruki symbol at the top and the words "Noritake China Japan" on a teal background	1931	D
33.	Shield-and-Wreath-under-Crown + the words "Noritake Bone China Japan"	1935	E
34.	the word "Noritake" above Azalea blossoms + the words "AzaleaPatt." and "Handpainted Japan" plus a design number or numbers	1934	E
35.	"Noritake China" + "Handpainted" above the Maruki symbol; "Nippontokikaisha Ltd" (printed as just 2 words) + "Nagoya, Japan" below it	1935	D
36.	"Noritake China" above a wreath with two characters in the center, and "Nippon Toki Kaisha" below; green and multi-color versions are known	1935	D
37.	same as the above but with additional Chinese/Japanese characters and no words in English	1935	D
38.	Noritake + M-with-Banner-and-Crown + Handpainted + Japan; red and multi-color versions known	1940	E
39.	same as above, but no "Handpainted"	1940?	E
40.	the Maruki symbol plus the abbreviation "N.T.K." (Nippon Toki Kaisha) plus the words "Bone China Japan"	1940	E?
41.	same as above but without the word "Japan"	1940	D
42.	Double-Laurel-Wreath-and-Bow, with "Noritake China" above + "Japan" or "Made in Japan" in one line below + letter "M" in center; was used until 1953	1933	E
43.	Lacey-Double-Laurel-Wreath with "Noritake China" above + "Hand Painted" in a curved line plus "Japan" below + letter "M" in center	1933	E
44.0156	same as above + the words "Japanese Design Patent Applied For" in red; usually they are located some distance from the rest of the backstamp	1933?	E
47.	Maruki symbol within an arabesque pattern + "Noritake" in script above + Nippon Toki Kaisha in block letters below	1947	D
49.	the letters RC (for "Royal Crockery") within a complex wreath + Nippon Toki Kaisha in block letters below	1949	D
50.3	"Noritake" above the Maruki symbol plus "Nippon Toki Kaisha" below; in magenta; compare to 16.3	1949	D
OJ50.	"Noritake" above the Maruki symbol plus "Made in Occupied Japan" below	1949	E
51.	"Noritake" above the Maruki symbol plus "Japan" below	1949?	E
52.	"Noritake" above the Maruki symbol plus "Foreign" below; used for items sent to Great Britain	1954	E
54.	Noritake + Maruki-in-Wreath + Made in Japan; generally seen on items exported to Australia and New Zealand	1933	E
55.	Maruki-in-Wreath + Bone China + Nippon Toki Kaisha (does not have the word "Noritake"); known in magenta, gold and black	1940	D
56.15	Maruki-in-Wreath + Bone China + Nippon Toki Kaisha (in black) + Made in Japan (in red) (does not have the word "Noritake")	1940?	E?
58.	Maruki-in-Wreath (and nothing else); green and red versions are known	1935	E

63.	Double-Laurel-Wreath-and-Bow, with "Noritake China" above + "Japan" or "Made in Japan" in one line below + letter "N" in center	1953	D+E
64.	Bowl-in-Wreath + Bone China + Nippon Toki (no "Kaisha")	1946?	D
65.	Bowl-in-Wreath + Bone China + Nippon Toki Kaisha + Japan; in all black or multi-color	1946?	D?
66.	Bowl-in-Wreath + Bone China + ® + Japan	1980	D+E
67.	Bowl-in-Wreath + Bone China + Nippon Toki Kaisha (no Japan or Made in Japan)	1946	D
68.	"Noritake" above + "Japan" below the Okura symbol	1968	E
69.	the word "Noritake" in script with a relatively large letter "N" and no accent on the letter "e" + the word Japan in block letters; in several colors; other words are often placed so near this backstamp they seem to be a part of it (e.g., see 69.9)	1950	E
69.9 (ani-mates)	the word "Noritake" in script with a relatively large letter "N" and no accent on the letter "e" + the word Japan in block letters; in this instance, the words "ani-mates" (in lower case block letters) and "designed by Kiyotada Itoh" appear also; printed on a paper label glued to the item	1978	D+E
70.	Noritake Bone China Japan in script; ignores edition numbers and similar details; such information usually will be noted in captions in parentheses after the backstamp number	1950?	E
71.	Noritake in script + Bone China A Limited Edition (of some number) in block letters + Japan; usually the edition size will be noted in captions in parentheses after the backstamp number	1950?	E
72.	N-in-Wreath-with-Bow + Bone China + ® + Japan	1986	D
74.	N-in-Wreath-with-Bow + ® +Japan (ignores variations due to two tiny dots in the wreath of some versions)	1968	D+E
AP75.	Special backstamp used only for merchandise that used Arnold Palmer's name (gives edition size)	1975	E
76.	N-in-Wreath (no bow) + Nippon Toki Kaisha + Japan	1955	D
77.	N-in-Wreath (no bow) + Nippon Toki Kaisha (but no Japan)	1955?	D?
78.	N-in-Wreath (no bow) + Studio Collection + Bone China + Japan	1976	D
86.	Noritake Legacy Philippines	1977	E

Backstamp **M.0**

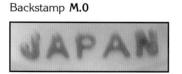

Backstamp **J.0**

Backstamp **J.0 (Chikaramachi)**

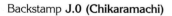

Backstamp **J.0w (30040)**
(Chikaramachi)

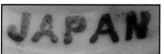

Backstamp **J.1**

Backstamp **J.2**

Backstamp **J.5**

Backstamp **JDP.0**

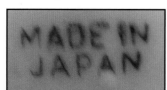

Backstamp **MIJ.0**

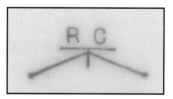

Backstamp **MIJ.1**

Backstamp **MIJ.1w**

Backstamp **MIJ.2**

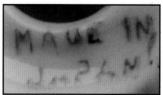

Backstamp **MIJ.2**

Backstamp **06.0**

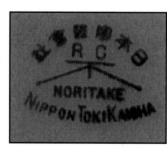

Backstamp **07.0**

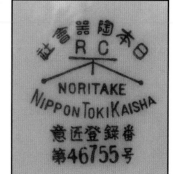

Backstamp **07.0 (46755)**

Backstamp **07.3**

Backstamp **14.0 (39539)**

Backstamp **16.0**

Backstamp **16.4w (25920)**

Backstamp **07.7**

Backstamp **15.1**

Backstamp **A16.1**

Backstamp **16.7**

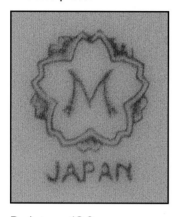

Backstamp **13.0**

Backstamp **15.01**

Backstamp **16.1**

Backstamp **18.0**

Backstamp **13.1**

Backstamp **15.01 (44046)**

Backstamp **16.3**

3.13 Backstamp **16.4**

Backstamp **19.0**

Backstamp **14.0**

Backstamp **19.1**

Backstamp **C20.1**

Backstamp **C23.1**

Backstamp **ML21.1**

Backstamp **19.1**

Backstamp **C21.0**

Backstamp **C23.5**

Backstamp **24.1**

Backstamp **19.2**

Backstamp **C21.5**

Backstamp **MC25.2**

Backstamp **25.0**

Backstamp **21.0**

Backstamp **C22.0 (30040)**

Backstamp **RC25.2**

Backstamp **RC26.0**

Backstamp **RC26.2**

Backstamp **25.1**

Backstamp **26.0**

Backstamp **27.1**

Backstamp **28.1 (Roseara)**

Backstamp **29.1 (19322)**

Backstamp **26.1**

Backstamp **27.2**

Backstamp **29.0 (23920)**

Backstamp **29.1 (29812)**

Backstamp **26.8**

Backstamp **27.3**

Backstamp **29.1**

Backstamp **27.0**

Backstamp **28.1**

Backstamp **29.7 (20056)**

Backstamp **31.7**

Backstamp **32.456**

Backstamp **33.056**

Backstamp **34.1**

Backstamp **35.1**

Backstamp **36.0**

Backstamp **36.056**

Backstamp **37.056**

Backstamp **38.1**

Backstamp **38.019**

Backstamp **39.019**

Backstamp **40.3**

Backstamp **41.3**

Backstamp **42.056**

Backstamp **43.056**

Backstamp **44.0156**

Backstamp **47.056**

Backstamp **49.456**

Backstamp **50.3**

Backstamp **OJ50.3**

Backstamp **51.3**

Backstamp **56.15**

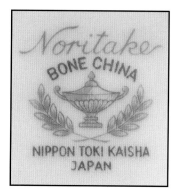

Backstamp **65.019**

Backstamp **68.7**

Backstamp **52.7**

Backstamp **58.0**

Backstamp **65.5**

Backstamp **69.3**

Backstamp **54.0**

Backstamp **58.1**

Backstamp **66.57**

Backstamp **69.9 (ani-mates)**

Backstamp **55.3**

Backstamp **63.056**

Backstamp **67.019**

Backstamp **70.7 (Fifth Edition)**

Backstamp **70.7 (Mother's Day 1976 Third Edition One of 2,800)**

Backstamp **55.5**

Backstamp **64.019**

Backstamp **71.7**

Backstamp **72.7**

Backstamp **74.7**

Backstamp **76.3**

Backstamp **77.3**

Backstamp **74.5**

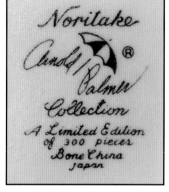

Backstamp **AP75.5**

Backstamp **76.7**

Backstamp **78.9**

Backstamp **86.5**

Part Two

Introduction

Although there are some very important materials in Part One of this book, Part Two definitely is the heart and soul of it. It is where most users of this book will spend most of their time. Accordingly, every effort has been made to organize the materials so that readers can quickly and easily find what they want. Because of this, I have begun, in previous versions of this introduction, by summarizing the organizational principles used in creating the chapters, the pages in them and the captions for the photos on them. I do provide that information but only after discussing certain apparent trends in the way some Art Deco era Noritake fancyware items were decorated. I hope some readers will use the ideas that I am about to present as they look through Part Two of this book.

The views presented here are the product of numerous discussions involving several collectors over a period of years. Frequently, these ruminations were presented in the pages of *Noritake News* (*the* quarterly newsletter for collectors of and dealers in Noritake fancyware; if you would like more information about it, write to me at Schiffer Publishing). A few of these ideas were presented in my 2002 Noritake book, but only in passing and with little explanation (see pp. 146, 244, 263-264). This viewpoint pertains to a special kind of Noritake set, a type that I and others often refer to as a *conceptual set*. In the years after this notion was first introduced (in March of 1999), some collectors have added to the fun of their hobby by attempting to assemble conceptual sets. Others enjoy trying to identify such sets by finding the relevant items in the pages of books that show Noritake fancyware. It is this latter exercise that led to this discussion being placed here at the start of Part Two. Some readers, I hope, will want to search for conceptual sets in this book. As it happens (but it is no accident), quite a few are shown in it.

Conceptual sets

We can best begin to explain what is meant by the term "conceptual set" if we contrast it with another more familiar type of set—a "functional set." Functional sets consist of items that belong together because they need to be and usually are *used* together. Many examples of such sets are shown in this book, particularly in Chapters C and T (appropriately enough, these are the only chapters of the book with the word "set" in the title). A few functional sets are shown in several other chapters—e.g., Chapter A (smoke sets), B (salad sets), D (dresser sets), P (serving sets) and Z (name card sets).

By contrast, *conceptual sets can be defined as items that belong together because they all share or exhibit certain ideas or concepts that apparently were used by those who decided how they were to be decorated*. At this point, an example will be helpful so please look at photo P2.1.

For reasons to be spelled out shortly, the three items shown in that photo constitute one type of "conceptual set," although not the only or even the best type. When looking at the items like those shown in the photo, one almost immediately notices some of their qualities or characteristics. For example, it may be noticed that the most prominent colors (yellow, red-orange and green) are quite different. Or one may focus on the fact that the items (two 6.5"w basket bowls and one 6.5"h vase) are not all the same shape or type. They do, however, have a common motif: a diamond-shaped floral landscape, although the skies are different colors.

P2.1 An example of a "conceptual set." Vase, 6.5"h. Trays, 6.63"w. Backstamps (all): 27.1.

In this example, the common motif does *partly* explain why I consider those items to be a conceptual set but it must be emphasized immediately that *many conceptual sets do not have the same motif* (we will return to this point shortly). Although it may seem puzzling at first, a feature that tells us, in this case and many others, that these items constitute a conceptual set is that the main colors are different. Indeed, the items in most Noritake conceptual sets probably have different dominant (or prominent) colors. For example, an important and also rather common color combination for a three-item conceptual set is blue, green and tan (or orange) luster. The frequently seen non-luster combinations include red (or orange), yellow, and blue (or green) and blue, green and orange.

Sometimes, on first inspection, a three-item Noritake conceptual set may appear to have only two prominent colors. An excellent example of such a set is shown in photo P2.2. These plates have named motifs that most collectors know as (from left to right): The Spanish Lady, Daisy, and The Peach Hat Lady. I (and others) think they constitute a conceptual set. But you may want to question this, especially if you have noticed already that two of these plates have tan luster rims while the Daisy plate rim is blue luster. Given the guidelines discussed so far, shouldn't we expect one of these plates to have a green luster rim? Well yes, we should expect it but we may not always find exactly what we expect. But then you may ask, if there is no green rim, how can this be a valid conceptual set?

P2.1 An example of a "conceptual set." Plates. 6.25"dia. Backstamps (all): 27.1.

At least four reasons can be advanced in support of the proposition that these plates constitute a conceptual set. The items share or exhibit (1) a common artistic style as well as common (2) painting techniques, (3) size and (4) motif components. As for these motif components, some may object in this case because only two of the ladies are wearing very big hats. Although true, the lady without a hat does have hair that looks very much like a big hat. Moreover, big sweeping curved lines (that create a fan and two hats) are central to all three of the motifs. There is also a possible fifth reason and, interestingly, it takes us back to the "three different prominent colors" principle. In the areas delimited by the big sweeping curved lines, there are three different prominent colors: red, orange and green.

We also know that not all conceptual sets consist of three items. Some sets have four items (an excellent example is shown in B.438 on p.101 of *Noritake Fancyware A to Z*). Others have just two (a fine example is shown in B.254 on p.59 of *Collecting Noritake A to Z*). I would not be all that surprised to learn that some Noritake conceptual sets have more than four items, but the most common number appears to be three.

At this point, we cannot say for certain why it is three or why certain color combinations are common. A plausible suggestion for the number three has to do with the role of that number in western aesthetics. In painting, for example, triangular arrangements of key elements offer powerful aesthetic advantages to the artist. As for the color combinations, I thought initially that the colors in a conceptual set typically would be blue, green and tan because those are the colors of one of the most distinctive features of the Noritake fancyware from the 1920s—the frequently seen luster finishes. As with all theories, however, this idea has had to be modified in light of new facts. Thus, while blue, tan and green probably are by far the most common combination in three-item *luster* Noritake conceptual sets, when non-luster paints were involved, many more combinations apparently were used. The

items shown in photo P2.1 illustrate this, as do several others in this book.

Two additional points about conceptual sets can be made here using the example shown in the photo above. First, in the prototypical or ideal conceptual set, all the pieces will be the same type of item. Thus, the set shown in photo P2.1 is not prototypical. It would be, however, if the three items shown were either identically shaped vases or basket bowls. That the photo above does not show such a "perfect" conceptual set is simply due to happenstance. The collectors who have the items in this photo do not happen to have a red-orange basket bowl with the appropriate motif; neither do they have the yellow and green versions of the red-orange vase. I used that less than ideal conceptual set in this discussion in part so I could show that the "they should be the same type of item" rule is not a rigid one.

Second, I used this particular conceptual set to show that *we may use our ideas about conceptual sets to **predict** the existence of Noritake fancyware items that we have never seen!* Such predictions are, of course, one of the most basic reasons for creating any theory. A good theory should enable its users to make good predictions. Given the items shown in the photo above and with what has been said so far about conceptual sets, we can fairly confidently predict that there is a red-orange basket bowl like the yellow and green ones. As it happens, I have seen an example of it (but this is *not*, please note, why I said that there should be one; that claim was derived from the logic of the theory). By the same token, we can also say that yellow and green versions of the red-orange vase should exist. To the best of my recollection, however, I have not seen either the green or yellow version of that vase. Even though we know for certain that a "perfect" three-item conceptual set involving these colors and the diamond-shaped floral landscape does exist (the basket bowl version), we *cannot assume* that the other two vases needed for that version of the conceptual set actually were made. Instead, we must wait to see whether or not the missing items for it are found. As has been noted, however, this is why we should be interested in a theory like this. Because of it, (a) we know we should be on the lookout for the missing vases, (b) we know almost exactly what they will look like (which helps in the hunt for them) and (c) we will be able to appreciate the extra-ordinary significance of an item that might otherwise seem fairly ordinary had we encountered it without the benefit of the theory.

As was noted above, it is extremely important to remember that not all conceptual sets have identical or nearly identical motifs (such as the diamond-shaped floral landscapes in the example we have been considering). This is because items in these sets only need to express some common idea(s) or concept(s) and, as can easily be imagined, this can be done in several ways. In this book, a good example of such a multi-motif conceptual set is the group of three vases without handles shown in photo V.434. By themselves, the three luster colors (blue, orange and green) and the uniform size and shape of the vases are facts that should lead one to at least consider whether these items might be a conceptual set. But the color combination alone will not settle the matter. For example, what if the blue vase had a traditional floral motif, the orange vase a Deco geometric one and the green vase had an elaborately costumed lady much like the one we see in the photo? As I think is probably obvious, it would be difficult to say how such diverse motifs are related conceptually. In short, *the motifs in a conceptual set can be different but they must be related conceptually and it should be possible to describe or state what factors or features forge the relationship.* In the case of the motifs on the vases shown in V.434, all three are ladies who are (a) about the same size, (b) standing in comparable ways and, most significantly, (c) are costumed dramatically (if not outrageously) in a similar style. This plus the other features noted (vase shape and three different luster background colors) make it almost certain that these vases are a conceptual set.

It is possible, however, that the vases in V.434 are not a *complete* conceptual set. There could be more Noritake vases that fit with the ones shown there. In my opinion (and it is only that; it is not a fact), I do not think such vases exist and so I also think the items shown in V.434 *do* constitute the *complete* set. To eager collectors, this should be disappointing news. Why? Because vases like the ones being discussed are excellent, highly sought after examples of the genre; collectors would only benefit if there were other different but related members of the set. To fit into the set, the others not yet discovered would have to be the same size and shape. Also, they *should* ideally have luster background colors other than the ones in the set shown in V.434 and they should feature other ladies in different but stylistically similar costumes.

This discussion has not exhausted the subject (and hopefully not the reader, either!). My more modest goal has been to alert collectors and dealers to the existence of such sets and to encourage them to search for them. The most important place to search, of course, is "out there" wherever you go in your search for collectible Noritake. But another very important place to search is right in this book. When you do this, do not limit yourself to examining photos that show three items (of which there are quite a few in this book). In the first place, some of the conceptual sets in this book are shown in three separate photos (hint: look in Chapter P). In the second place, some photos show two items from a three item conceptual set. In fact, incomplete sets may be the most interesting ones to identify because (as was noted above), the general ideas we have been discussing will enable you to predict what the missing member or members of the set should look like. Making such predictions is useful because once you have a good mental image of the item, even if it is one you have never seen before, your chances of spotting it in a crowd of other items in your neighborhood "Junque Shoppe" will increase. But, third, you should also consider looking for such sets using all the available books on Noritake collectibles. If you do this, you probably will find that some of the more interesting two-, three- and four-item conceptual sets are shown one item at a time in different books. Putting these sets together in your mind will increase your chances of being able, one day, to put them together on a shelf in one of your display cases.

Chapter organization

The chapters in Part Two are designated by letters and sequenced alphabetically. Doing this makes the book easier to use as a reference tool. The chapter-designating letters have mnemonic value. This enables users to quickly figure out and then easily remember where things of interest to them are likely to be in this book. For example, if you happened to be interested in seeing photographs of Noritake **a**shtrays, you would turn to Chapter A. If **b**owls were your interest, then the relevant chapter would be B but if it were **v**ases that you wanted to look at, then you would flip to Chapter V. Because the chapter letter designations and chapter names are shown as a running head on every other page of Part Two, one generally can locate the relevant chapter within seconds just by flipping pages.

This is only part of the story, however. This book is not organized like a dictionary with each piece located in a sequence determined by the first letter of the term used to identify, name or describe it. Rather, the pieces shown have been grouped into a small number of fairly broad and mostly functional categories, one to each chapter of Part Two. For example, the photographs in Chapter A are not of ashtrays alone. Included in it are photographs of all items with a close functional link to smoking. This fact is signaled by the full title of the chapter: "Ashtrays and Other Items Related to Smoking." Accordingly, in addition to ashtrays, Chapter A has photographs of cigarette boxes, holders and jars, as well as humidors, match holders, smoke sets, tobacco jars and more.

At the beginning of each chapter there is an alphabetic list of all the kinds of items that will be found in it, as well as the page numbers on which photographs of those pieces are located. Experience shows that, within just a few minutes, most users of the book can learn the few particulars of this organizational approach that need to be mastered. If all else fails, however, there is an index that pinpoints the location of desired material of all kinds.

Caption organization

In this book, the captions have four basic components sequenced as follows: description (including photograph number), dimensions, backstamp number and *approximate* retail value range. These components are largely self-explanatory but certain matters are reviewed briefly here.

Description (including photograph number)

The words at the start of the caption indicate what an item is. Usually, these words will be the same or very nearly the same as one of the subgroup categories given in the list at the start of each chapter. If there are additional comments about the items shown, they usually are inserted at this point in the caption. The description portion of the caption also includes the photo numbers. These are given within parentheses: e.g., (A.212).

As you have no doubt noticed, these "numbers" are actually a combination of letters and numerals, with the letter given first. That letter is the one used to designate the chapter in which the photograph appears. Next are numerals that designate the sequential position of the photograph in that chapter. Thus, a number such as "A.212" would designate the two hundred twelfth photograph in the "A" or "Ashtrays and Other Items Pertaining to Smoking" chapter<u>s</u>. The letter "s" in the last word of the previous sentence is emphasized because the photograph numbers for each chapter begin with the number after the last one in the same chapter of my most recent previous book on Noritake collectibles. Because the last photo of Chapter A in my previous book was A.211, the first photograph of Chapter A in this book is A.212.

Sometimes there is more than one photograph of a piece, usually to show the back or to show certain details more clearly. The photograph number of these pictures has a letter that follows the sequence numerals. Thus, a photograph number like "A.212A" indicates a photograph that is a variant of photograph "A.212." In this instance, as the full caption in Chapter A indicates, A.212A shows what the ashtray shown in A.212 looks like when the cover is removed. Had there been two alternate photographs, the second one would have been designated as A.212B.

Dimensions

One should not assume that other pieces like the ones shown in this book will always have exactly the same dimensions. There are at least three reasons for this. For one thing, variations in size can be expected when items are made of porcelain, both because of the character of porcelain and because of the mass-production techniques used to create these particular porcelains. For another, some Noritake fancywares were made in several distinct sizes but in some photographs these differences are not at all obvious. Thus and for example, you could have an 8" version of a bowl that, in this book, happens to be the 6" version. Finally, measurement errors are unavoidable even though, in creating this book, every reasonable effort was made to be as precise as possible about dimensions.

Dimensions are given in decimal form to the nearest eighth inch (.13"). When necessary, measurements were rounded up. Normally, the first dimension given is overall, or greatest, height (indicated by the letter "h"). This is followed by overall or greatest width ("w") and, if available or useful, *front-to-back* depth ("d"). *Diameter* is generally given only for basically flat and *truly* round items such as certain plates without handles, powder puff boxes and the like. Height sometimes is not given for basically flat items such as these. For basically flat objects that are *nearly* round, such as cake plates with small handles, the dimensions given are "width" (at the handles or the widest point) *and* "depth" (or, if one prefers, as the "other width" across the plate at the widest point *without* the handles). Finally, when they were available, the dimensions of all items in multi-item sets are provided.

Backstamp

The identity of most of the backstamps on pieces shown in this book is indicated by the word "Backstamp:" followed by a number of some sort. The meanings of these numbers are discussed in Chapter 3. The backstamp on most of the pieces shown in this book will be one of three types. The most common, by far, is what collectors know as an "M in Wreath" type. These are all designated by a number beginning with 2; indeed, the vast majority of these will be 27.0 or 27.1. The other two very common backstamps are the "Maruki" type (usually those designated by the number 16.0, 16.1, etc.) and the "Cherry Blossom" type (designated by the number 19.0, 19.1, etc.).

The number to the right of the decimal indicates the color(s) of the backstamp. The most commonly seen colors, by far, are green (.0) and red or maroon (.1). Thus, a caption with the phrase "Backstamp: 27.1." should be read as indicating that the item shown has a red or maroon "M in Wreath" backstamp. Other colors found on other backstamps are designated by other numerals to the right of the decimal. A complete list of the color codes used in the backstamps is presented in Chapter 3. Color photos of these backstamps are also to be found there.

Value

The last numbers in the caption indicate the *approximate retail value range* in current U.S. dollars of near-mint versions of the item(s) shown in the photograph. For example, numbers such as $120-150 would indicate an *approximate retail value range* of U.S. $120.00-$150.00. Sellers should not presume that the top end of the range is usually the best asking price; similarly, buyers should not expect that they can usually purchase items at the bottom end of the range. Sometimes, both ends of the range are *not* indicated numerically. Instead, just the lower end is given. For the trinket dishes shown in D.265, for example, putting "Each, $800+" at the end of the caption indicates that one should expect to see a retail price of *at least* $800.00 on *each* item. This method of indicating value is reserved for rather unusual and highly desirable items which, so far (and alas), have been seen only rarely in the Noritake collectibles market.

It is impossible for these value designations to be any more than a *rough guide* to the current retail value of any of the pieces. Many factors, such as individual preferences and changing fashions among collectors as well as the condition of the piece can have a significant impact on the utility of this information. In this book, the value figures given presume the items are in "near-mint" condition (one rarely if ever sees a truly "mint" piece of pre-War Noritake porcelain). A major factor that can be expected to influence value (or "price") is the manner in which an item is sold—e.g., whether by live auction, Internet auction, at an antique show, at a garage or tag sale, privately and so on. For all these reasons, neither the publisher nor author is responsible for gains or losses that may occur when using or quoting the opinions expressed on these matters in this book.

Chapter A
Ashtrays and Other Items
Pertaining to Smoking

In this chapter are photographs of items directly related to smoking. Photos of the following specific kinds of items are arranged in the order shown:

Ashtrays in figural form or with figural elements (pp.45-46)
Ashtrays without figural elements (pp.46-50)
Ashtrays with match holders (p.50)
Cigarette boxes (p.51)
Cigarette holders (pp.52-53)
Cigarette jars (pp.53-54)
Humidors (p.54)
Match holders (p.55)
Pipe stand (p.55)
Smoke sets (p.56)
Tobacco jars (p.56)

As with all the chapters of this book, there are more items worthy of comment than there is space to discuss them. That is why I mention only a dozen or so items even though many others deserve a comment. I begin with ashtrays in figural form or with figural elements. As has been the case for several years, smoking items with figural elements are in great demand. Perhaps the most unusual such item in this chapter is shown in A.213, followed closely by the one in A.212. Until the item in A.213 came along, I had seen neither a figural donkey nor an ashtray in the shape of the one that this donkey is sitting on in my 20+ years of rather serious involvement with the collecting of Noritake. The coppery luster glaze on the donkey is also quite unusual for Noritake fancyware of this (or any) period. The golf ball ashtray shown in A.212, a post-war item, is unusual and quite striking. It too is an item that I had not seen until very recently. It is rather large and cleverly designed.

Of the other ashtrays, the two shown in the A.219 photos are quite spectacular and very unusual. The motif on the left tray reminds one very much of work by Picasso. The motif on the right is utterly different in feel, figuratively and, due to the use of enameling, literally. Both trays are striking also for the way the design is developed in the back of the piece. The ashtray in A.223 is very nice but, by itself, not particularly rare or striking. I mention it, however, because of the humidor shown in A.261, which the ashtray clearly matches. With these two items, one is forced to consider at least two questions, neither of them having answers at this point. First, were there other smoking-related items with this motif (e.g., a tray or match holder)? Second, did Noritake humidors from the 1920s generally have matching ashtrays? In the years ahead, we can hope to learn the answer to these questions as collectors scour the Internet auction sites and their favorite antique shows. Finally, for the ashtrays, take a look at the two shown in A.229 and A.230. To me, they seem closely related in both subject matter and style. Once again, these items raise interesting questions that as yet we are unable to answer. First, were these trays part of a set? For example and keeping in mind comments about "conceptual sets" made above in the introduction to Part Two, was there perhaps a third tray with a different bird and a green luster trim? Or, second, were these trays part of different smoke sets, each with other items having the motifs shown?

Each of the four figural lady cigarette jars shown in A.255 is striking but, the four together are very impressive indeed, since these are rather hard-to-find items. Another example of the one on the left was shown in A.193 in my 2002 book. I could have asked for it to be edited out, but I couldn't do that to such an elegant piece. The most unusual one of the four is the white one with the red dot motif. The backstamp (RC26.0) is unusual also. It was registered in Bombay in 1926 and was used on items originally exported to India. Although smaller and a lone item, the "Betty Boop" motif on the cigarette holder shown in A.249 is very striking. Seeing it gives one hope that there is an entire smoke set with that motif out there somewhere.

Like the other items being mentioned here, the humidors shown in A.265 and A.266 are unusual in several ways. Until very recently, few collectors had seen the motif and shape of the one shown in A.265. Curiously, other items shaped like it have since been seen but neither one is a humidor. How do we know the others are not humidors? Because the inside of the handles of the lids of humidors are hollow. The space holds a piece of moistened sponge that helps keep the tobacco moist. The lids of those other spherical covered boxes have solid handles. The humidor in A.266 has what most would consider a superb Deco motif. The match holder in A.267 has considerable charm and, with its plaid decoration, is sure to appeal to many collectors. The match holder shown in A.269, on the other hand, has a somewhat mysterious quality and is a very unusual shape. Wouldn't you like to see the rest of the smoke sets that these two items were part of originally?

One of the rarest (and cutest) items in the chapter is the figural pipe stand shown in the two A.270 photos. Surely (or so it would seem), Noritake items like this were decorated in a dozen different ways. And yet, so far, I have seen only three. Some, I suppose, may think that is a gloomy comment, but I see it as offering hope for collectors wanting such an item for their collection. At least a few others *must* be out there; we just need to find them. The smoke set shown in A.271 has been selected for comment here simply because of its unusual design and *very* striking coloring; yellow is always easily noticed (or difficult to ignore) as well as relatively uncommon for Noritake items from the 1920s. The Egyptian theme of the smoke set in A.272 is intricate and elegant. It also is rare for items from the Noritake era; such motifs are far more common on items from the Nippon era—i.e., prior to 1921 for pieces exported to the United States. The last item to be mentioned is the tobacco jar shown in A.275. The motif is unusual and the backstamp (RC25.2) is another of those used on items destined for India.

Figural ashtray (A.212). 4.5"h x 3.75"w. Backstamp: 77.3. $100-150.

Alternate view (A.212A) of A.212 showing green removable tray insert.

Figural ashtray (A.213). 3.0"h x 5.75"w x 4.13"d. Backstamp: 27.1. $450-750.

Ashtray (A.214) with figural element. 3.0"h x 4.88"dia. Backstamp: 27.0. $180-320.

Ashtray (A.215) with figural element. 2.5"h x 4.25"w. Backstamp: 27.0. $350-450.

Ashtray (A.216) with figural element. 2.75"h x 3.5"w x 3.38"d. Backstamp: 27.1. $250-350.

Alternate view (A.216A) of ashtray in A.216.

Ashtray (A.217) with figural element. 2.5"h x 4.25"w x1.13"d. Backstamp: 27.0. $300-400.

Detail (A.219B) of left ashtray in A.219.

Ashtrays (A.218) with figural element. Bird, 1.88"h x 3.75"w x 3.25"d. Swan, 1.88"h x 3.63"w. Backstamps: C23.5. Each, $20-40.

Detail (A.219C) of right ashtray in A.219.

Ashtrays (A.219). 3.0"h x 5.13"w. Backstamps: 27.1. Left, $200-300; right, $300-500.

Back view (A.219A) of ashtrays in A.219.

Ashtray (A.220). 2.75"h x 4.88"w. Backstamp: 27.0. $120-220.

Ashtray (A.221). 1.13"h x 6.63"w. Backstamp: 27.0. $300-400.

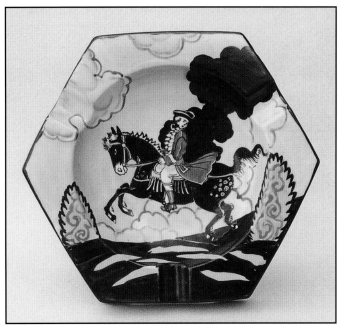

Ashtray (A.222). 1.25"h x 5.88"w x 5.88"d. Backstamp: 27.0. $150-250.

Detail (A.221A) of A.221.

Detail (A.222A) of A.222.

Ashtray (A.223). 1.25"h x 5.13"w. Backstamp: 27.0. $70-120.

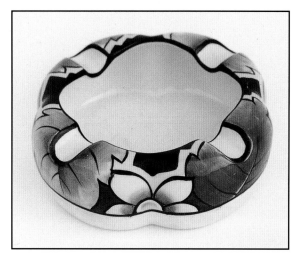

Ashtray (A.224). 1.75"h x 4.5"w. Backstamp: 27.0. $40-60.

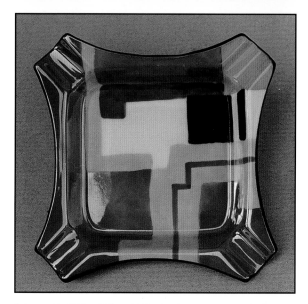

Ashtray (A.227). .63"h x 4.5"w. Backstamp: 16.0. $80-120.

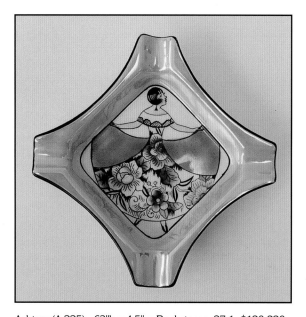

Ashtray (A.225). .63"h x 4.5"w. Backstamp: 27.1. $120-220.

Ashtray (A.228). .63"h x 4.5"w. Backstamp: 27.0. $90-160.

Ashtray (A.226). .63"h x 4.5"w. Backstamp: 27.1. $140-240.

Ashtray (A.229). .63"h x 4.5"w. Backstamp: 27.0. $90-160.

Ashtray, spade (A.230). .38"h x 3.25"w x 3.0"d.
Backstamp: 27.0. $50-90.

Ashtray, heart (A.231). .38"h x 3.0"w x 3.0"d.
Backstamp: 27.0. $50-90.

Ashtray, diamond (A.232). .38"h x 3.75"w x 3.38"d.
Backstamp: 27.0. $50-90.

Ashtray, club (A.233). .38"h x 3.25"w x 3.0"d.
Backstamp: 27.0. $50-90.

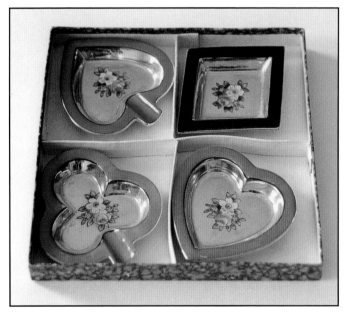

Ashtray set (A.234) with original box. Spade, .38"h x 3.25"w x
3.0"dia. Heart, .38"h x 3.0"w x 3.0"dia. Diamond, .38"h x 3.75"w x
3.38"dia. Club, .38"h x 3.25"w x 3.0"dia. Backstamps: 27.0. Set as
shown, $100-140.

Ashtrays (A.235). .88"h x 3.25"w x 3.0"d. Backstamps: 27.1. Pair,
as shown, $20-40.

Ashtrays (A.239) with figural match holders. *Left*, 1.88"h x 5.38"w x 5.75"d. Backstamp: 27.0. *Right*, 1.88"h x 4.88"w x 4.75"d. Backstamps: 27.1. Each, $70-120.

Ashtrays (A.236). .88"h x 3.25"w x 3.0"d. Backstamps: 27.1. Pair, as shown, $20-40.

Ashtray (A.240) with match holder. 2.0"h x 3.75"w x 2.63"d. Backstamp: 27.1. $40-80.

Ashtray (A.237). .75"h x 4.38"w. Backstamp: 19.0. $20-30.

Ashtray (A.238) with match holder. 2.5"h x 3.75"w. Backstamp: 27.1. $250-350.

Ashtray (A.241), with match holder? 1.38"h x 2.88"w x 2.63"d. Backstamp: J.1. $20-30.

Cigarette box (A.242). 3.75"h x 4.38"w x 4.25"d. Backstamp: 36.0. $40-80.

Cigarette box (A.243). 1.63"h x 4.25"w x 3.38"d. Backstamp: 27.1. $100-180.

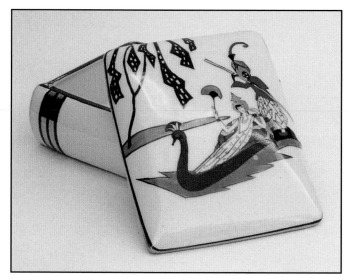

Cigarette box (A.244). 4.13"h x 3.63"w x 1.75"d. Backstamp: 29.1. $190-290.

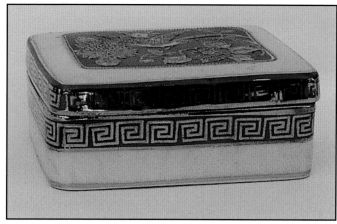

Cigarette box (A.245). 1.5"h x 3.62"w x 2.88"d. Backstamp: 27.1. $90-140.

Top view (A.245A) of A.245.

Cigarette box (A.246). 1.5"h x 3.5"w x 2.75"d. Backstamp: 27.1. $90-140.

Cigarette holder
(A.247). 3.88"h x
3.25"w x 2.63"d.
Backstamp: 29.1
(33519). $60-100.

Cigarette holder (A.250). 3.88"h x 2.5"w x 2.38"d.
Backstamp: 25.1. $50-100.

Cigarette holder (A.248).
3.75"h x 2.5"w x 2.38"d.
Backstamp: 27.1. $200-
300.

Cigarette holder (A.249).
3.75"h x 2.38"w.
Backstamp: 27.1. $200-
300.

Cigarette holder (A.251). 4.0"h x 2.63"w x 2.0"d.
Backstamp: 27.0. $50-100.

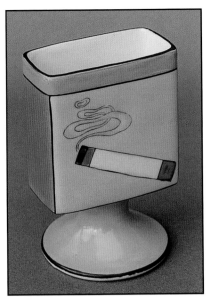

Cigarette holder (A.252). 3.88"h x 2.5"w x 2.38"d. Backstamp: 54.0. $40-80

Cigarette jar (A.255). 6.25"h x 3.0"w. Backstamp: 19.0. $500-900.

Cigarette holders (A.253). *Left*, 4.0"h x 3.25"w x 2.63"d. *right*, 3.0"h x 2.63"w x 2.0"d. Backstamps: 27.1. *Left*, $120-190, *right*, $90-140.

Cigarillo jar (A.256). 4.5"h x 2.75"w. Backstamp: 27.1. $400-600.

Cigarette jars (A.254). 5.75"h x 2.75"w. Backstamps: *second from left*, RC26.0; *others*, 29.0 (25920). Each, $750-1300.

Cigarette jar (A.257). 5.0"h x 2.88"w. Backstamp: 27.0. $100-150.

Cigarette jar (A.258).
4.88"h x 3.5"w.
Backstamp: 27.0.
$400-650.

Humidor (A.261).
6.25"h x 5.25"w.
Backstamp: 27.0.
$350-550.

Humidor (A.259).
7.0"h x 5.38"w.
Backstamp: 27.0.
$350-500.

Humidor (A.262).
5.5"h x 4.38"w.
Backstamp: 25.1.
$100-200.

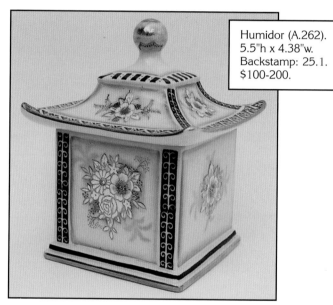

Humidor (A.260). 6.5"h x
4.5"w. Backstamp: 27.0.
$500-700.

Humidor (A.263).
5.25"h x 3.88"w.
Backstamp: 27.0.
$300-500.

Humidor (A.264). 5.25"h x 4.63"w. Backstamp: 25.1. $200-300.

Humidor (A.265). 4.5"h x 5.5"w x 3.5"d. Backstamp: 27.1. $300-450.

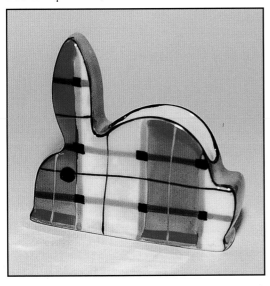

Match holder (A.266). 2.5"h x 2.75"w x .75"d. Backstamp: 27.1. $170-270.

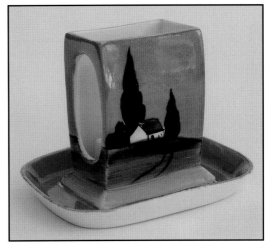

Match holder (A.267). 2.5"h x 3.88"w x 3.0"d. Backstamp: 27.0. $40-70.

Match holder (A.268). 2.88"h x 3.0"w x 2.38"d. Backstamp: MIJ.1. $50-80.

Pipe stand (A.269). 2.88"h x 3.75"w. Backstamp: 19.0. $350-$450.

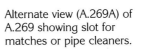

Alternate view (A.269A) of A.269 showing slot for matches or pipe cleaners.

Smoke set (A.272). Tray, .63"h x 6.88"w x 2.75"d. Match holder, 2.13"h x 2.38"w x 1.0"d. Cup, 2.38"h x 2.25"dia. Backstamps: Tray, unmarked; match holder, MIJ.1; cup, 27.1. $420-520.

Smoke set (A.270). Tray, .5"h x 8.5"dia. Ashtray, 1.25"h x 4.75"w x 4.5"d. Tobacco jar, 4.0"h x 3.75"w x 3.63"d. Match box holder, 2.75"h x 2.13"w x 1.5"d. Backstamps: all 27.0, except matchbox holder, MIJ.0. $290-430.

Tobacco jar (A.273). 6.5"h x 4.25"w. Backstamp: 27.0. $250-350.

Tobacco jar (A.274). 5.25"h x 3.63"w. Backstamp: RC25.2. $300-400.

Smoke set (A.271). Tray, .63"h x 7.13"w x 4.88"d. Ashtray, .5"h x 2.88"w x 1.75"d. Match holder, 2.13"h x 2.38"w x 1.0"d. Backstamps: 58.0. $550-750.

Tobacco jars (A.275). 3.75 "h x 3.5"w. Backstamps: *Left,* 27.0; *right,* 27.1. *Left,* $150-250; *right,* $200-300.

Detail (A.271A) of box lid in A.271.

Chapter B
Bowls and Boxes

With photos of well over 200 different Noritake bowls as well as a few boxes, this is the largest chapter in this book. This is also the most complex chapter, with more than two dozen bowl types and subtypes. Even so, it is *easy* to become proficient at locating quickly any particular kind of bowl of interest. This is because the bowl types and subtypes are defined using readily identified features. The materials in this chapter are clustered into two main groups: ***Bowls*** and ***Boxes***. Each of these main groups is divided into two subgroups. For Boxes, the subgroups are **Figural Boxes** and **Other Boxes**. Because there are so few items in these subgroups (alas), there is no need to divide them further. (Some Noritake boxes, however, can be found in other chapters—especially Chapters A and D.)

For Bowls, the two subgroups are **General Purpose Bowls** and **Special Purpose Bowls**. Because there are so many bowls, each of these subgroups is divided further into various bowl "types." These bowl types, as well as various subtypes ("kinds") and sub-subtypes ("varieties") to be mentioned shortly, are created and named with reference to a *few* distinctive features (e.g., the number of handles or the basic shape). In this book there are four named *types* of General Purpose Bowls and ten named *types* of Special Purpose Bowls. These *types* have descriptive names that, in the list below, are numbered and appear in Italics to make them easier to find. Because the four types of General Purpose Bowls come in *many* different shapes and sizes, they were divided into twelve named kinds (or subtypes). One of these subtypes ("sided bowls with two handles and no feet") is very large and so it, and it alone, is divided into named sub-subtypes (or "varieties"). As can be seen in the list, there are four named "varieties" of sided bowls with two handles and no feet.

Here is how to locate, quickly and easily, any *bowl* in this chapter. First, consider whether the bowl of interest has some specific or special purpose, function or name (e.g., is it a nut or punch bowl, or a covered bowl or compote). If you think it is a special purpose bowl, check below to see if your name for it is among the ten types of Special Purpose Bowls (including "various other"). If the bowl of interest is one of these *types*, simply turn to the pages indicated and, within a minute or two, you should know whether there is a photo in this book of a Special Purpose Bowl like the one of interest to you.

If the bowl of interest is *not* a Special Purpose Bowl (or is not in the list of Special Purpose Bowl types), turn to the list of General Purpose Bowls. To find a particular General Purpose Bowl in this book, first determine what *type* it is. *All of the General Purpose Bowl types in this book are based on one simple, easy-to-see feature: the number of handles*. Once the *type* has been identified, there are two

options. Either turn directly to the pages that show that *type* of bowl or see if the item of interest falls within one of the bowl sub-types listed. Because there are so many bowls in virtually all of the basic General Purpose Bowl *types*, it usually will be worthwhile to identify the subtype of the bowl.

I use from one to three features to define Bowl *subtypes*. Often, the most telling of these features is the *type of handle*. Thus, some bowl subtypes are defined with reference to whether they have loop (basket) handles or handles in a figural form. A second feature that is sometimes used to designate a bowl subtype is whether the bowl has *feet (or legs)*. Because these two features (handles and feet) are very obvious, it usually is *very* easy to place any Noritake bowl in a subtype that is defined with reference to them. The third feature that is used to define bowl subtypes is the basic *shape* of the bowl or, or, more precisely in many cases, the shape suggested by the *rim* of the bowl.

Some bowl shapes are simple and obvious—e.g., round bowls or square (four-sided) ones—and fortunately, many if not most Noritake bowls have such easily recognized, nameable shapes. Some Noritake bowls, however, have shapes that are neither easily defined nor readily named. Therefore, and in an effort to keep things as simple as possible, the list below utilizes only four named bowl (or bowl *rim*) shapes: (1) oval (or ovoid), (2) pointed, (3) round and (4) sided. Almost all of the bowl examples in the first three of these four bowl shapes can usually be recognized easily and reliably. Typical users of this book, therefore, are likely to feel that nearly all of the bowls shown in the sections featuring these three shapes were classified correctly.

With regard to *sided bowls* (i.e., bowls with sides, or with rims that give the bowl the appearance of having sides), however, we may sometimes expect less agreement. Fortunately, this potential difficulty tends to arise within only one of the sided bowl subtypes: sided bowls with two handles and no feet. As it happens, however, the Noritake Company made *many* such bowls. With a little experience, though, you will see how and why bowl location decisions were made and will thus be able to find things rapidly.

In summary, *all the types, kinds and varieties of General Purpose Bowls listed below are designated with reference to some combination of these features:* **type and/or number of handles, the presence or absence of feet or legs, and basic shape**. Once you have identified the subtype (or in some cases, the sub-subtype) of a General Purpose bowl that is of interest, simply turn to the pages indicated. Within a minute or two, you should know if the kind of bowl you are interested in is shown in this book. Nevertheless, if a bowl of interest is not shown in the first section of the chapter you think it will be in, consider other possible locations within the chapter. If, after following these steps, a photo of the bowl of interest is not found, it probably is safe to conclude that one like it is not shown in this book. With these introductory remarks in mind (or at least at hand), you are now well positioned to make good use of the complete list, which follows, of all the groups, types, kinds and varieties of bowls and boxes in this chapter.

Bowls

Some truly magnificent items are shown here. Experienced Noritake collectors will argue, correctly in my view, that the various boxes at the end of the chapter are the most deserving of accolades and, in due course, I will comment on some of them. Before we get to those masterpieces, how-

ever, I am eager to offer some words of praise for a few of the other very fine items from the "bowl" category. Of necessity, given the size of the chapter, the items to be mentioned in this way will be only a fraction of those that warrant special comment. As it happens, we can begin right at the beginning because the items shown in the first few photos are rather unusual and elegant. The shape of the item in B.568 is not particularly rare; two more excellent bowls in that shape are shown in the next photo. What sets that item apart from the others is the unusual and very Deco color combination used to decorate it. The floral motif in the center is also very well conceived, I think, as is the similar floral motif on the bowl on the right of B.569. The next two photos, B.570 and B.571 are an interesting pair. They show items that are very similar in general shape (they do differ in size) and both bowls feature cottage motifs that are fairly rare (indeed, I have not seen other items with these cottages). The motif in B.571 is especially desirable because it fits well within a type that collectors refer to as a "Deco cottage scene" (the floral cluster in the bottom front of the motif adds support to that claim). The scene in B.570, while not at all Deco (at least as I see things), is rather uncommon; it also is unusual in that it covers the entire surface of the bowl and appears to be a totally free-hand painting.

Noritake fancyware from the 1921-1931 period is famous, justifiably, for the use of bold primary colors. This is what causes us to take special note of the bowl shown in B.574—it features nothing but soft pastel shades and as such is most unusual (although we do see it again on the compote in B.735). The three bowls shown in B.576 bring us sharply back to the bold colors we are more accustomed to seeing on Noritake fancy china from this period. They are mentioned, however, because they constitute the first example, in this chapter, of a conceptual set (for more on this, see the Introduction to Part Two of this book). Readers are encouraged to see if they can find others in this chapter. And to make it more interesting (because three item conceptual sets are relatively easy to identify when shown in a single photo as in the case of B.576), keep your eyes peeled for *incomplete* conceptual sets. A very nice example is presented in B.579. Surely there is a third bowl like these but in another color. But what color? Will it be green (my guess) or red?

The very unusual bowl shown in B.578 could almost be a Rorschach test. I see a yellow and red bird near a strange flower. What do *you* see? The big mystery with the shallow but oh so elegant bowl shown in B.580 is how the decorators managed to create those thickly gilded palm trees. Surface texture on Noritake fancyware items (as with the bowl shown in B.580) is something that many collectors are attracted to, and for good reason. One of the most dramatic and elegant items shown in this chapter (and it is not mine) features texture quite prominently. I refer to the stunning bowl shown in B.587. Whimsy is another quality in a motif that appeals to many collectors and a nice example, I think, is shown in B.599. I know of few Noritake items that feature green peppers. This bowl is unusual also for its background color and is striking for the way the rim has been decorated. On very rare occasions, a bowl (or other item) can be as important for the backstamp on it as for any other feature. A superb example is the unusual bowl shown in B.606. Although the figural bird is striking, it is not particularly rare; the painted motif is far more unusual in my experience. But what sets this bowl apart is that it has *two* backstamps and one of them, the green one, is very rarely seen outside of Japan (it was used on items intended for their domestic market). Since only the lower Maruki backstamp is under the glaze, I will guess that this item was intended originally for Great Britain but was, for some reason, withdrawn from a shipment and marked again so that it could be sold in Japan. At the moment, this bowl resides in the United States. Another bowl with an important backstamp is shown in B.670. That backstamp tells us the item it is on was originally exported to Indonesia!

Sometimes, collectors do a classic "double take" when they see two items that, at first seem to be the same, but that are not. The two bowls shown in B.610 and B.611 are a good example. I will not describe how they are different (or similar); you can do that easily enough. Do notice, though (and you will need to look carefully), that the molded leaf *is* present in both bowls. Nearby, in B.614 and B.615, there are two other bowls that will need close attention to appreciate fully; there is a subtle pattern in the white luster. In this chapter as well as others in this book, close attention needs to be given at times to the dimensions reported in the captions. For example, consider the magnificent bowl shown in B.616. Experienced collectors will know this shape but, if they are not careful, they will think the item shown is about 7 or 8 inches wide because that is the most common size. This one, however, is more than 10 inches wide and, as such, is a veritable *giant*. The bowls shown in B.647, B.648 and B.649 are also instances of this, as are those shown in B.655 and B.656.

Continuing with the "sometimes you have to look closely" issue, consider the unusual item shown in B.618 which *is* correctly placed with the other bowls with one side handle. Do you see the handle? At least two other one-handled bowls deserve comment: B.626 for its unusual rim treatment (the backstamp tells us it was originally exported to Australia), and B.631 for being in this chapter at all. This is not because it is undeserving but, rather, because a similarly shaped item was shown in photo Z.26 of *Collecting Noritake A to Z* where it was called, quite *in*correctly, a silent butler (or crumb catcher). Shortly after that book came out, a collector in Texas informed me that she had once seen a set of six such bowls on a shelf in an antique store. So, although it is still only a guess (hopefully one that is not as bad as my previous one regarding an item like this), it may be that these bowls were part of a set that included a master bowl of some sort, but *what do you suppose it looked like*?

One of the most spectacular items in this book, let alone this chapter, is the "Sisters Bowl" shown in B.638 (disclaimer: it is not mine). No further comment on it is necessary; the photos provide all the evidence one needs to justify my claim. Although not quite in the same league as the Sisters Bowl just mentioned, the *elegant* bowl in B.659 must not be missed; the bowl shown in the very next photo is also quite striking. Two other bowls not far from the two just mentioned warrant comment as well. I refer to the items shown in B.663 and B.664. The use of gold on the item in B.663 is wonderfully extravagant; the rarely seen floral motif plus the geometric components of the motif in B.664 make it a gorgeous Deco item. Now, have a look at the bowl shown in B.682. Although it certainly is attractive enough, one still may wonder why I should want to mention it when there are so many other bowls in this chapter that are decorated just as compellingly. The key is the backstamp. Far too many collectors continue to believe that a Cherry Blossom backstamp means that the item is less well decorated than items with an M-in-Wreath backstamp. Sometimes this may be so but, just as often, it will not be so, as the bowl under discussion convincingly demonstrates. The last General Purpose bowl that I will say anything about is one of the more unusual items in the book. I refer to the bowl shown in B.686—an item originally exported to Australia (where it is still).

For some collectors, the phrase "Noritake relish dish" is virtually a synonym for "boring." Those harboring this attitude will be hard pressed to stick with it after they look at the relish sets shown in this book. The set shown in B.703 has both an unusual shape and an incredible floral motif. The one shown in B.705 has a more typical shape but it stands out because of its superbly executed motif in colors seldom seen on Noritake fancyware. Without the individual salts with the set in B.707, most of us would not know that the attractive bowl is a relish server. The relish bowl in B.708 is one of the very few items I have seen with a motif with the look of a needlepoint design. One of the wildest designs in this entire book is on the relish bowl shown in B.709 while B.710 shows a relish bowl in an unusual, very seldom-seen shape.

The two-piece Noritake centerpiece bowl that we see in B.722 has to be one of the most stunning in captivity. Howard Kottler, who liked to name Noritake motifs, called this one "Birch Exotica Landscape" (his item with the motif was a vase). The prize for the most stunning one-piece centerpiece bowl, at least for this book, probably should go to the one shown in B.726. It is a fantastic piece. The prize for the strangest piece in this book could well belong to the item shown in B.731. What in the world of the 1920s did one do with such a thing (other than hide it)? A compote (or tazza) at the other end of the spectrum is the one shown in B.733. The discovery of King Tut's tomb, in 1922, may well have led to the decision to use this motif. The covered bowls shown in photos B.744-B.747 are of interest for the way they illustrate the wide stylistic range that can be seen on a single blank.

All of the nut bowls and nut bowl sets shown in this book are rather unusual. Two of them (B.752 and B.753) are noteworthy because one seldom sees the individual nut dishes shown with them; this is particularly true of the set in B.752 (I know of no other one, though surely there must be many of them out there). The bowl shown in B.754 is deceptive; it looks like it could be one of the small individual nut bowls but it is, in fact, a rather large master bowl. Very probably it came, originally, with six little individual bowls in the same shape. Be sure to take note of the marvelous molded-in-relief surface and peanut feet shown in B.754A.

I have just about concluded that the best Noritake salad bowl sets were exported to Australia. As evidence, consider the dramatic ones shown in this book with backstamps showing that they were sent there, originally (B.755, B756 and B.759). One of the more unusual sets, however (and one that is also rather impressively decorated) is the set shown in B.760. Two very unusual sets pertaining to fruit are shown in this part of the book. B.762 shows a bowl (from Australia) for draining washed fruit; the items shown in B.764 are individual fruit bowls that, clearly, originally went with a larger bowl shaped much like (if not exactly the same as) the bowl shown in B.763.

The Noritake boxes shown in this book are so rare and so striking (especially B.766-B.770), there is hardly need for comment. They stand out for all who see them, whether or not they are Noritake collectors. I will note, however, that we are still quite puzzled as to the function of the figural boxes. The

discovery of the item on the left in B.767A does, however, lend credibility to the suggestion that the covered box is for cigarettes and that the other item is an ashtray, even though there is no cigarette rest (this is discussed in Chapter D, also). The box shown in B.771 is, in shape, just like the humidor shown in A.264 but, unlike that item, the lid handle on the box in B.771 is solid so there is no place to install a damp sponge (to keep tobacco from drying out). It is thus a covered box, not a humidor.

There are many wonderful items in this chapter that I have said nothing about. I hope you can appreciate that space constraints have forced me to be extremely selective. I am very confident, however, that you can and will enjoy all the other items in this chapter on your own. When it comes to the "Bowls and Boxes" chapter, there truly is something here for everyone. Enjoy.

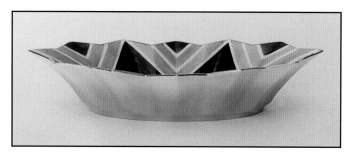

Pointed bowl (B.568). 1.63"h x 8.5"w x 4.25"d. Backstamp: 27.1. $100-200.

Alternate view (B.568A) of B.568.

Pointed bowls (B.569). 2.38"h x 8.5"w x 4.25"d. Backstamps: 27.1. Each, $80-180.

Pointed bowl (B.570). 2.5"h x 10.75"w. Backstamp: 19.1. $100-200.

Detail (B.570A) of B.570.

Pointed bowl (B.571). 1.88"h x 7.38"w.
Backstamp: 25.1. $100-200.

Round bowl (B.573). 3.5"h x 10.0"w. Backstamp: 19.0. $60-100.

Detail (B.571A) of B.571.

Round bowl (B.574). 2.75"h x 8.5"w. Backstamp: 27.0. $40-80.

Pointed bowl (B.572). 3.13"h x 10.5"w x 10.25"d. Backstamp:
27.1. $60-120.

Alternate view (B.574A) of B.574.

Round bowl (B.575). 2.75"h x 8.75"w. Backstamp: 19.0. $40-80.

Round bowls (B.576). 3.0"h x 9.0"w. Backstamps: 27.0. Each, $40-90.

Round bowl (B.577). 2.75"h x 8.25"w. Backstamp: 27.0. $40-80.

Round bowl (B.578). 2.75"h x 8.25"w. Backstamp: 27.0. $80-120.

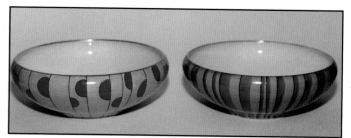

Round bowls (B.579). 2.75"h x 8.25"w. Backstamps: 27.0. Each, $50-90.

Alternate view (B.579A) of B.579.

Round bowl (B.580). 2.38"h x 10.0"dia. Backstamp: 16.0. $120-220.

Detail (B.580A) of B.580.

Round bowl (B.581) with 3 feet. 2.75"h x 6.75"w.
Backstamp: 27.1. $30-60.

Round bowl (B.583) with 3 ball feet. 2.63"h x7.63"dia. Backstamp:
27.0. $60-110.

Alternate view (B.581A) of B.581.

Alternate view (B.583A) of B.583.

Round bowl (B.582) with 3 feet. 2.75"h x 6.75"dia.
Backstamp: 27.0. $40-80.

Three-sided bowl (B.584). 3.75"h x 6.75"w. Backstamp: 27.0. $40-90.

Four-sided bowl (B.585). 3.0"h x 9.5"w. Backstamp: 27.1. $30-50.

Alternate view (B.585A) of B.585.

Alternate view (B.584A) of B.584.

Six-sided bowl (B.586). 2.0"h x 10.25"w x 9.5"d. Backstamp: 27.0. $40-80.

Eight-sided bowl (B.587). 3.0"h x 9.5"w. Backstamp: 27.1. $220-290.

Ten-sided bowl (B.589). 2.88"h x 8.0"w. Backstamp: 27.1. $40-80.

Eight-sided bowl (B.588). 2.25"h x 7.38"w. Backstamp: 27.1. $30-50.

Alternate view (B.588A) of B.588.

Twelve-sided bowl (B.590). 2.5"h x 9.88"w. Backstamp: 19.1. $30-50.

Four-sided bowl (B.591) with four feet. 2.38"h x 9.38"w. Backstamp: 27.0. $30-60.

Alternate view (B.591A) of B.591.

Six-sided bowls (B.592) with three feet. 1.63"h x 5.38"w. Backstamps: *left*, 27.1; *right*, 27.0. Each, $20-30.

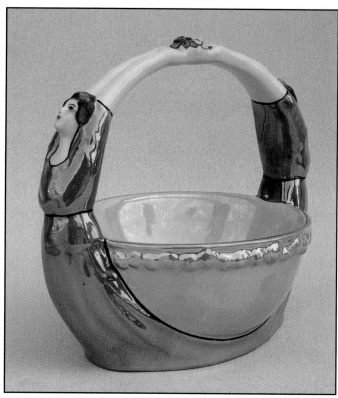

Gemini (basket) bowl (B.593). 6.0"h x 6.5"w x 5.0"d. Backstamp: 19.2. $1000-1500.

Basket bowls (B.594). 5.88"h x 7.75"w x 4.88"d. Backstamps: 27.0. Each, $40-80.

Basket bowls (B.595). 5.5"h x 6.5"w x 4.25"d. Backstamps: 27.0. Each, $40-80.

Basket bowl (B.596). 5.5"h x 7.63"w x 7.0"d. Backstamp: 27.0. $20-40.

Alternate view (B.598A) of B.598.

Basket bowl (B.597). 4.38"h x 6.5"w x 5.38"d. Backstamp: 27.1. $80-130.

Basket bowl (B.599). 3.38"h x 7.88"w x 4.88"d. Backstamp: 27.1. $90-130.

Basket bowl (B.598). 4.0"h x 7.5"w x 7.38"d. Backstamp: 27.1. $50-100.

Basket bowls (B.600). 3.0"h x 7.5"w. Backstamps: 27.0. Each, $30-50.

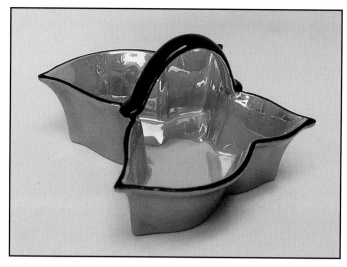

Basket bowl (B.601). 3.25"h x 5.63"w x 4.75"d. Backstamp: 27.1. $60-80.

Basket bowl (B.603). 2.38"h x 7.0"w x 3.5"d. Backstamp: 19.2. $20-40.

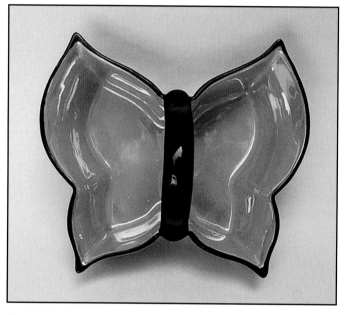

Alternate view (B.601A) of B.601.

Basket bowl (B.604). 3.5"h x 6.63"w x 4.25"d. Backstamp: 27.1. $40-90.

Basket bowls (B.602). 3.5"h x 7.38"w x 5.38"d. Backstamps: 27.0. Each, $60-80.

Basket bowls (B.605). 5.0"h x 5.0"w x 4.13"d. Backstamps: 27.1. Each, $50-80.

Bowl (B.606) with figural handle.
2.75"h x 6.75"w x 5.5"d.
Backstamps: 06.0 *and* 16.7.
$120-190.

Backstamps
(B.606A) on the
bowl shown in
B.606.

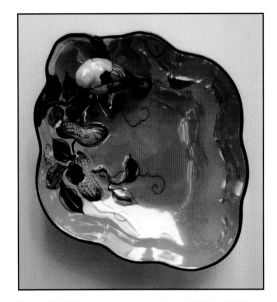

Bowl (B.609) with figural handle. 1.88"h x 9.0"w x
7.63"d. Backstamp: 19.1. $90-190.

Bowl (B.607) with figural handle. 4.0"h x 7.5"w x 5.5"d.
Backstamp: 27.0. $150-250.

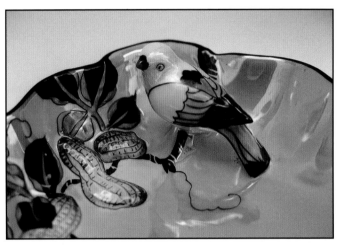

Detail (B.609A) of B.609.

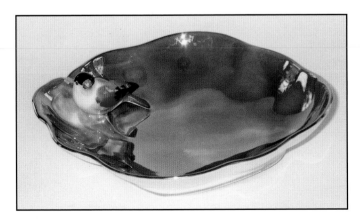

Bowl (B.608) with figural handle. 2.38"h x 8.0"w x 7.0"d.
Backstamp: 27.0. $250-400.

Bowl (B.610) with figural handle. 1.5"h x 6.0"w x 5.75"d.
Backstamp: 27.0. $40-60.

Bowl (B.611) with figural handle. 1.5"h x 6.0"w x 5.75"d.
Backstamp: 27.0. $40-60.

Bowl (B.614) with figural handle. 2.25"h x 6.38"w x 4.88"d.
Backstamp: 27.1. $20-30.

Bowls (B.612) with figural handles. 1.5"h x 6.0"w x 5.75"d.
Backstamps: 27.1. Each, $40-60.

Bowls (B.615) with figural handles. 2.25"h x 6.38"w x 4.88"d.
Backstamps: 27.1. Each, $20-30.

Bowls (B.613) with figural handles. 1.88"h x 6.75"w x 4.63"d.
Backstamps: 27.1. Each, $30-40.

Bowl (B.616) with one handle. 3.38"h x 10.25"w x 9.63"d. (Note:
These dimensions are correct. This is an unusually large version of
this bowl.) Backstamp: 27.0. $120-200.

Bowl (B.617) with one handle. 2.13"h x 9.25"w x 8.0"d. Backstamp: 27.0. $60-90.

Bowl (B.620) with one handle. 2.25"h x 8.0"w x 7.5"d. Backstamp: 27.1. $20-40.

Bowl (B.618) with one handle. 2.5"h x 9.63"w. Backstamp: 27.1. $40-70.

Bowls (B.621) with one handle. 1.5"h x 6.63"w x 6.25"d. Backstamps: *Left,* 25.1; *right,* 27.0. Each, $20-30.

Bowl (B.619) with one handle. 2.25"h x 8.0"w x 7.5"d. Backstamp: 27.1. $30-60.

Bowls (B.622) with one handle. 1.25"h x 6.0"w x 5.63"d. Backstamps: 27.0. Each, $20-30.

Bowl (B.623) with one handle. 1.25"h x 6.0"w x 5.63"d.
Backstamp: 27.1. $30-40.

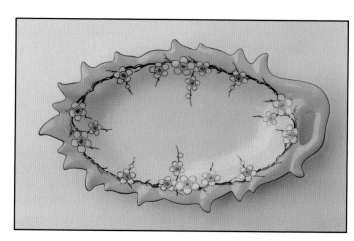

Bowl (B.626) with one handle. 1.25"h x 8.0"w x 4.75"d.
Backstamp: 54.0. $30-50.

Bowl (B.624) with one handle. 1.5"h x 6.5"w x 6.0"d.
Backstamp: 27.0. $10-20.

Bowl (B.627) with one handle. 1.63"h x 6.88"w x 5.75"d.
Backstamp: 27.0. $10-20.

Bowls (B.625) with one handle. 1.5"h x 5.88"w x 5.5 "d.
Backstamps: *Lower right,* 26.0; *others,* 27.1. Each, $10-20.

Bowls (B.628) with one handle. 1.5"h x 6.25"w x 4.63"d.
Backstamps: 27.0. Each, $10-20.

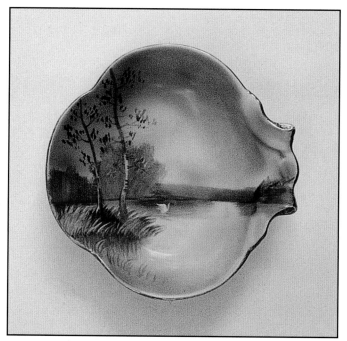

Bowl (B.629) with one handle. 1.75"h x 6.0"w. Backstamp: 27.0.
$10-20.

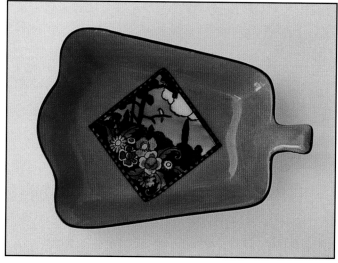

Bowl (B.631) with one handle. 1.88"h x 6.25"w x 4.5"d.
Backstamp: 27.1. $20-40.

Bowl (B.630) with one handle. 1.5"h x 5.63"w x 4.75"d.
Backstamp: 26.0. $20-40.

Bowl (B.632) with one handle. 3.0"h x 5.88"w x 4.25"d.
Backstamp: 27.1. $40-80.

Bowl (B.633) with two figural handles (Sisters Bowl). 4.0"h x 8.0"w x 5.25"d.
Backstamp: 27.1. $2500+

Alternate view (B.633A) of B.633.

Top view (B.633B) of B.633.

Detail (B.633C) of B.633.

Bowl (B.634) with two figural handles.
"4.5h x 11.0"w x 9.0"d. Backstamp: 21.0. $200-300.

Detail (B.634A) of B.634.

Bowl (B.635) with two figural handles. 4.75"h x 11.13"w x 9.13"d. Backstamp: 16.4. $200-300.

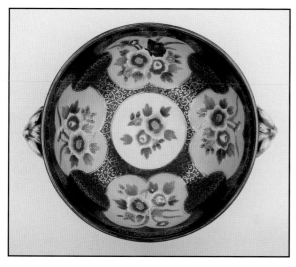

Top view (B.635A) of B.635.

Ovoid bowl (B.636) with two handles. 2.0"h x 8.13"w x 6.38"d. Backstamp: 27.0. $40-80.

Detail (B.636A) of B.636.

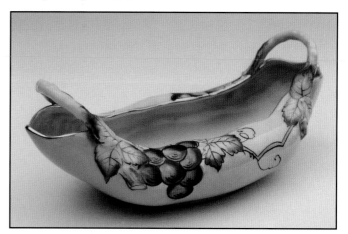

Ovoid bowl (B.637) with two handles. 3.5"h x 8.5"w x 4.5"d. Backstamp: 27.0. $90-180.

Ovoid bowl (B.638) with two handles on silver stand. Bowl, 1.5"h x 8.75"w x 6.25"d. Stand, 7.75"h x 9.5"w x 4.5"d. Backstamp: 16.4. $250-400.

Ovoid bowl (B.639) with two handles. 2.38"h x 9.75"w x 4.5"d. Backstamp: 26.0. $20-30.

Alternate view (B.639A) of B.639.

Alternate view (B.638A) of bowl in B.638.

Ovoid bowl (B.640) with two handles. 1.75"h x 10.5"w x 7.63"d. Backstamp: 27.1. $40-80.

Detail (B.638B) of bowl in B.638.

Detail (B.640A) of B.640.

Ovoid bowls (B.641) with two handles. 1.38"h x 6.25"w x 4.13"d. Backstamps: *Top left,* 27.1; *top right,* 26.0; *bottom,* 27.0. Each, $10-20.

Alternate view (B.643A) of B.643.

Ovoid bowls (B.642) with two handles. 1.63"h x 7.63"w x 4.63"d. Backstamps: 27.1. Each, $20-30.

Round bowl (B.644) with two handles. 3.5"h x 6.75"w x 6.63"d. Backstamp: 27.0. $10-20.

Round bowl (B.643) with two handles. 2.5"h x 6.75"w x 5.88"d. Backstamp: 27.0. $40-80.

Round bowl (B.645) with two handles. 2.0"h x 6.5"w x 5.0"d. Backstamp: 19.2. $20-30.

Round bowl (B.646) with two handles. 2.0"h x 7.38"w x 6.63"d. Backstamp: 27.1. $40-70.

Round bowl (B.649) with two handles. 1.75"h x 8.13"w x 7.13"d. Backstamp: 27.0. $30-40.

Round bowl (B.647) with two handles. 2.0"h x 10.5"w x 9.0"d. Backstamp: 27.0. $40-70.

Round bowls (B.650) with two handles. 1.88"h x 8.13"w x 7.13"d. Backstamps: *Lower left,* 29.1 (39557); *others,* 27.1. Each, $20-40.

Round bowl (B.648) with two handles. 1.88"h x 9.38"w x 8.0"d. Backstamp: 27.1. $40-70.

Round bowls (B.651) with two handles. 1.5"h x 7.25"w x 6.38"d. Backstamps: 27.0. Each, $10-20.

Round bowl (B.652) with two handles. 1.5"h x 8.38"w x 7.5"d. Backstamp: 27.0. $30-40.

Round bowl (B.655) with two handles. 2.0"h x 8.13"w x 7.25"d. Backstamp: 27.1. $40-60.

Round bowls (B.653) with two handles. 1.63"h x 8.38"w x 7.38"d. Backstamps: *Upper left,* 27.1; *upper right and lower left,* 27.0; *lower right,* 19.0. Each, $20-40.

Round bowls (B.656) with two handles. 1.75"h x 6.88"w x 6.0"d. Backstamps: *Upper left* and *lower right*, 27.1; *others*, 27.0. Each, $10-30.

Round bowl (B.654) with two handles. 1.63"h x 8.63"w x 6.75"d. Backstamp: 27.0. $20-30.

Round bowls (B.657) with two handles. 1.25"h x 5.38"w x 5.88"d. Backstamps: 25.1. Each, $10-20.

Round bowl (B.658) with two handles. 1.38"h x 5.25"w x 4.75"d. Backstamp: 27.0. $20-40.

Four-sided bowl (B.660) with two handles. 1.75"h x 8.75"w x 7.5"d. Backstamp: 27.0. $140-190.

Four-sided bowl (B.659) with two handles. The blue bird is a Hyacinth Macaw; the pink one a Moluccan Cockatoo. 2.13"h x 10.88"w x 9.63"d. Backstamp: 27.0. $350-450.

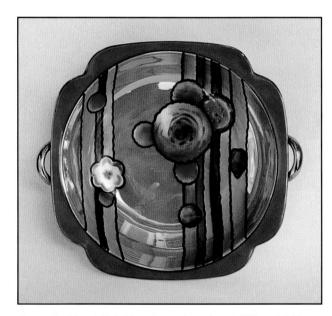

Four-sided bowl (B.661) with two handles. 1.88"h x 8.38"w x 7.38"d. Backstamp: 27.1. $40-70.

Detail (B.659A) of B.659.

Four-sided bowl (B.662) with two handles. 2.0"h x 9.13"w x 7.5"d. Backstamp: 27.0. $40-60.

Four-sided bowl (B.663) with two handles. 2.38"h x 9.0"w x 6.63"d.
Backstamp: 16.0. $150-200.

Four-sided bowl (B.665) with two handles. 1.75"h x 7.63"w
x 5.5"d. Backstamp: 25.1. $40-90.

Detail (B.665A) of B.665.

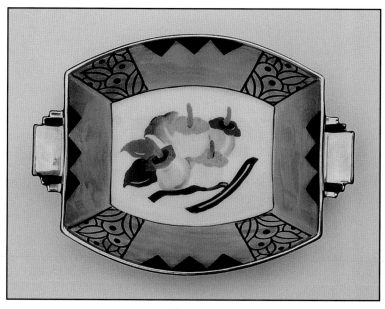

Four-sided bowl (B.664) with two handles. 1.75"h x 7.63"w x 5.5"d.
Backstamp: 25.1. $150-200.

Four-sided bowl (B.666) with two handles. 3.0"h x
6.25"w x 4.38"d. Backstamp: 16.0. $50-100.

Alternate view (B.666A) of B.666.

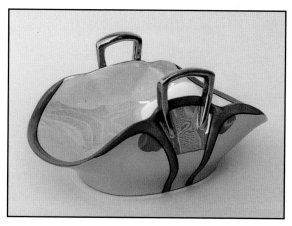

Four-sided bowl (B.667) with two handles. 3.25"h x 6.38"w x 4.38"d. Backstamp: 27.1. $10-20.

Four-sided bowl (B.668) with two handles. 2.0"h x 9.0"w. Backstamp: 27.1. $40-60.

Four-sided bowl (B.669) with two handles. 1.75"h x 6.0"w. Backstamp: 25.1. $30-40.

Four-sided bowl (B.670) with two handles. 1.75"h x 6.0"w. Backstamp: MC25.2. With this backstamp, $40-80.

Four-sided bowl (B.671) with two handles. 3.63"h x 9.38"w x 8.0"d. Backstamp: 27.0. $40-80.

Detail (B.671A) of B.671.

Four-sided bowl (B.672) with two handles. 2.5"h x 9.25"w x 8.0"d.
Backstamp: 27.0. $40-70.

Four-sided bowls (B.673) with two handles. 1.5"h x 5.5"w x 4.5"d.
Backstamps: *Top row*, 27.1; *bottom left*, 27.0; *others*, 25.1. Each,
$10-30.

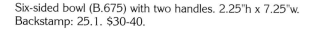

Six-sided bowl (B.675) with two handles. 2.25"h x 7.25"w.
Backstamp: 25.1. $30-40.

Six-sided bowl (B.674) with two handles. 2.0"h x 9.38"w.
Backstamp: 27.1. $90-160.

Detail (B.674A) of B.674.

Eight-sided bowl (B.676) with 2 handles 2.88"h x 8.25"w x 6.25"d. Backstamp: 15.1. $50-90.

Eight-sided bowl (B.679) with two handles 1.75"h x 7.88"w x 6.63"d. Backstamp: 27.0. $20-40.

Eight-sided bowl (B.677) with 2 handles 1.5"h x 11.0"w x 10.0"d. Backstamp: 19.1. $40-60.

Eight-sided bowls (B.680) with two handles 1.5"h x 6.0"w x 6.0"d. Backstamps: *Left,* 25.1; *right,* 27.1. Each, $30-50.

Eight-sided bowl (B.678) with two handles 2.63"h x 11.0"w x 10.25"d. Backstamp: 27.0. $30-50.

Eight-sided bowl (B.681) with two handles 1.88"h x 10.13"w x 9.13"d. Backstamp: 27.1. $80-120.

Eight-sided bowl (B.682) with two handles 1.88"h x 10.13"w x 9.13"d. Backstamp: 27.1. $80-120.

Eight-sided bowl (B.684) with two handles 1.5"h x 6.75"w x 6.25"d. Backstamp: 27.1. $90-180.

Eight-sided bowl (B.683) with two handles 1.75"h x 10.75"w x 10.38"d. Backstamp: 21.0. $30-50.

Detail (B.684A) of B.684.

Eight-sided bowls (B.685) with two handles 1.5"h x 6.88"w x 6.25"d. Backstamps: 27.1. Each, $20-40.

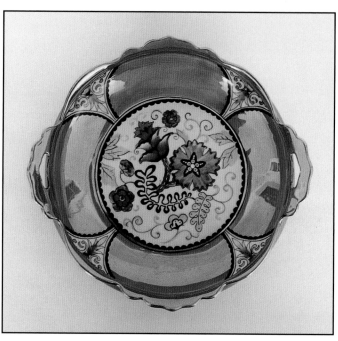

Alternate view (B.687A) of B.687.

Ten-sided bowl (B.686) with two handles. 2.5"h x 11.5"w x 8.5"d. Backstamp: 58.0. $200-300.

Bowl (B.688) with two handles and three feet. 2.5"h x 8.63"w x 7.0"d. Backstamp: 27.0. $30-50.

Bowl (B.687) with two handles and three feet. 3.5"h x 9.88"w x 9.38"d. Backstamp: 19.1. $50-90.

Alternate view (B.688A) of B.688.

86

Bowl (B.689) with three handles. 2.25"h x 9.25"w.
Backstamp: 27.0. $40-60.

Bowl (B.692) with three handles. 1.38"h x 7.25"w.
Backstamp: 27.1. $40-80.

Bowl (B.690) with three handles. 1.13"h x 5.75"w x 5.75"d.
Backstamp: 29.1. $30-50.

Bowls (B.693) with three handles. 1.25"h x 6.0"w.
Backstamps: 27.1. Each, $20-40.

Bowl (B.691) with three handles. 2.13"h x 8.5"w.
Backstamp: 27.1. $40-80.

Bowls (B.694) with three handles. 1.13"h x 6.0"w.
Backstamps: *Lower left*, 19.1; *others*, 27.1. Each, $20-40.

Bowl (B.695) with three handles. 1.63"h x 7.38"w x 7.38"d.
Backstamp: 27.1. $40-70.

Detail (B.695A) of B.695.

Bowl (B.696) with three handles. 1.38"h x 5.75"w.
Backstamp: 27.0. $20-40.

Bowl (B.697) with four handles. 3.25"h x 11.25"w x 8.63"d.
Backstamp: 27.1. $40-60.

Bowl (B.698) with four handles. 3.63"h x 8.0"w x 8.0"d.
Backstamp: 27.0. $30-50.

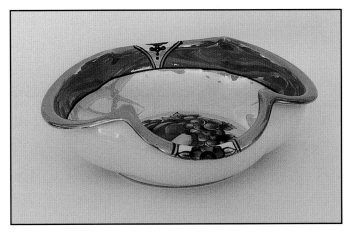

Bowl (B.699) with four handles. 2.38"h x 7.0"w x 6.13"d.
Backstamp: 19.1. $20-30.

Alternate view (B.699A) of B.699.

Bowl (B.700) with four handles. 2.25"h x 7.0"w. Backstamp: 27.0.
$20-40.

Bowl (B.701) with four handles. 2.38"h x 7.88"w x 7.88"d.
Backstamp: 27.1. $40-80.

Bowl (B.702) with four handles. 1.5"h x 6.0"w. Backstamp: 58.1.
$40-80.

Celery set (B.703). Celery bowl, 1.88"h x 12.5"w x 5.75"d. Individual salts, .5"h x 3.63"w x 2.25"d. Backstamps: 27.0. Set, as shown, $140-190.

Celery set (B.705). Celery bowl, 2.25"h x 12.63"w x 5.5"d. Individual salts, .75"h x 3.5"w x 2.0"d. Backstamps: 25.1. Set, as shown, $140-190.

Detail (B.703A) of B.703.

Celery set (B.706). Celery bowl, 2.5"h x 12.63"w x 2.38"d. Individual salts, 1.5"h x 2.38"w. Backstamps: 29.1. Set, as shown, $100-150.

Celery set (B.704). Celery bowl, 2.25"h x 12.38"w x 5.5"d. Individual salts, .63"h x 3.75"w x 2.25"d. Backstamps: 27.1. Set, as shown, $140-190.

Relish set (B.707). Relish bowl, 1.5"h x 7.25"w x 5.25"d. Individual salts, .38"h x 2.5"w x 1.63"d. Backstamps: 27.0. Set, as shown, $80-120.

Celery/relish bowl (B.708). 2.13"h x 12.0"w x 5.5"d. Backstamp: 27.1. $40-80.

Relish/fruit bowl (B.712). 1.5"h x 11.38"w x 4.0"d. Backstamp: 54.0. $40-80.

Celery/relish bowl (B.709). 2.0"h x 12.5"w x 5.75"d. Backstamp: 27.1. $60-90.

Celery/relish bowls (B.713). 2.5"h x 12.63"w x 5.25"d. Backstamps: 27.1. Each, $30-40.

Celery/relish bowl (B.710). 1.75"h x 12.5"w x 5.75"d. Backstamp: 25.1. $50-80.

Celery/relish bowl (B.711). 2.38"h x 12.75"w x 6.25"d. Backstamp: 27.0. $40-70.

Celery/relish bowl (B.714). 1.75"h x 10.88"w x 5.38"d. Backstamp: 27.0. $40-80.

Relish bowl (B.715). 3.0"h x 10.5"w x 8.0"d. Backstamp: 19.1. $20-30.

Center-handled serving bowl (B.718). 3.38"h x 8.75"w. Backstamp: 27.1. $30-50.

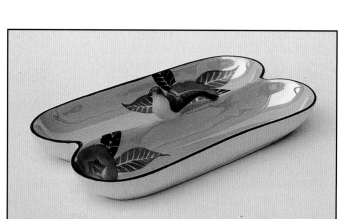

Relish bowl (B.716). 1.75"h x 6.5"w x 4.0"d. Backstamp: 27.0. $40-80.

Center-handled serving bowl (B.719). 3.0"h x 7.25"w. Backstamp: 27.1. $20-40.

Center-handled serving bowl (B.717). 4.38"h x 9.25"w. Backstamp: 19.0. $40-90.

Alternate view (B.717A) of B.717.

Center-handled serving bowl (B.720). 3.0"h x 7.25"w. Backstamp: 25.1. $20-40.

Center-handled serving bowls (B.721). 3.0"h x 7.25"w. Backstamps: 27.1. Each, $40-90.

Centerpiece bowl (B.722). 6.75"h x 11.88"w x 9.25"d. Backstamp (base only): 27.0. $400+

Alternate view (B.722A) of B.722.

Centerpiece bowl (B.723). 4.38"h x 11.88"w x 9.25"d. Backstamp: 19.1. $120-220.

Alternate view (B.723A) of B.723.

Child's cereal/porridge bowl (B.724). 1.25"h x 7.0"dia. Backstamp: 27.2. $40-60.

Detail (B.724A) of B.724.

Child's cereal/porridge bowl (B.725). 1.25"h x 7.0"dia. Backstamp: 27.2. $40-60.

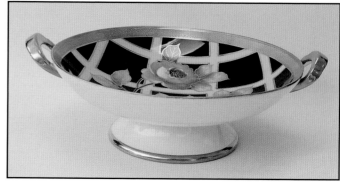

Compote (B.726) with two handles. 4.0"h x 11.38"w x 9.5"d. Backstamp: 27.0. $150-200.

Alternate view (B.726A) of B.726.

Detail (B.726B) of B.726.

Compote (B.727) with two handles. 5.0"h x 10.25"w x 8.13"d.
Backstamp: 27.0. $80-160.

Compote (B.728) with two handles. 2.63"h x 10.0"w x 7.63"d.
Backstamp: 19.1. $30-60.

Detail (B727A) of B.727.

Compote (B.729) with two handles. 2.5"h x 8.75"w x 7.0"d.
Backstamp: 27.0. $20-30.

Compotes (B.730) with two handles. 2.25"h x 6.88"w x 5.88"d.
Backstamps: 27.0. Each, $30-50.

Compote (B.731) with two handles. 5.25"h x 8.25"w x 5.63"d. Backstamp: 26.0. $20-30.

Compote or tazza (B.733) without handles. 6.75"h x 9.13"w. Backstamp: 27.0. $280-380.

Compote (B.732) with two handles. 3.13"h x 7.38"w x 5.5"d. Backstamp: 27.0. $30-40.

Detail (B.733A) of B.733.

Alternate view (B.732A) of B.732.

Compote (B.734). 6.88"h x 6.88"w. Backstamp: 27.1. $700+

Compote (B.735). 5.0"h x 7.0"dia. Backstamp: 27.0. $40-60.

Compote (B.736). 5.5"h x 11.88"w x 8.0"d. Backstamp: 16.0. $130-230.

Compote (B.737). 2.5"h x 7.88"dia. Backstamp: 27.0. $30-40.

Compote (B.738). 2.75"h x 6.5"dia. Backstamp: 27.1. $40-50.

Compote (B.739). 2.75"h x 6.5"dia. Backstamp: 27.1. $40-60.

Compotes (B.740). 2.75"h x 6.5"dia. Backstamps: 27.1. Each, $20-30.

Compote (B.741). 2.75"h x 6.5"w. Backstamp: 24.1. $30-50.

Covered bowls (B.742). 5.75"h x 7.0"w. Backstamps: *Left,* 27.1; *right,* 21.0. Each, $40-80.

Covered bowl (B.743). 4.88"h x 8.0"w x 6.25"dia. Backstamp: 27.0. $70-90.

Alternate view (B.742A) of left bowl in B.742.

Covered bowl (B.744). 4.5"h x 8.0"w x 6.25"d. Backstamp: 27.0. $800+

Covered bowl (B.745). 4.5"h x 8.0"w x 6.25"d. Backstamp: 27.0. $200-300.

Covered bowls (B.747). 4.5"h x 8.13"w x 6.38"d. Backstamps: *Left,* 21.0; *center,* 27.0; *right,* 27.1. Each, $40-80.

Alternate view (B.745A) of B.745.

Covered bowl (B.748). 5.0"h x 5.0"w. Backstamp: 19.0. $40-90.

Covered bowl (B.746). 4.88"h x 8.0"w x 6.25"d. Backstamp: 27.1. $100-150.

Covered bowl (B.749). 4.5"h x 4.0"w x 4.0"d. Backstamp: 27.0. $40-90.

Covered bowl (B.750). 4.5"h x 6.0"w. Backstamp: 27.0. $40-80.

Nut bowl set (B.753). Master bowl, 3.75"h x 8.0"w x 6.0"d. Individual bowls, 1.38"h x 3.5"w x 2.5"d. Backstamps: 27.1. Set shown, $100-150.

Nut bowl set (B.751). Master bowl, 3.75"h x 6.5"w. Individual bowls, 1.0"h x 2.0"w. Backstamps: 27.0. Set shown, $150-200.

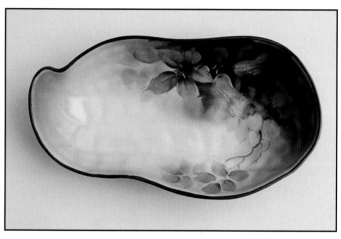

Nut bowl (B.754). 2.75"h x 8.13"w x 4.38"d. Backstamp: 27.0. $50-80.

Nut bowl set (B.752). Master bowl, 5.25"h x 7.0"w x 5.25"d. Individual bowls, 1.13"h x 2.75"w. Backstamps: master bowl, 27.1; individual bowls, MIJ.1. Set shown, $200-250.

Alternate view (B.754A) of B.754.

Salad bowl set (B.755). Bowl, 4.75"h x 10.5"w. Plate, 1.5"h x 10.5"w. Fork and spoon, 7.5"long x 1.88"d. Backstamps: 58.0. Set, as shown, $250-300.

Salad bowl set (B.758). Bowl, 4.38"h x 8.0"w. Plate, 1.5"h x 10.75"w. Fork and spoon, 7.25"long x 1.88"w. Backstamps: 27.1 (plate unmarked). Set, as shown, $180-280.

Salad bowl set (B.756). Bowl, 3.75"h x 7.88"w. Plate, 1.13"h x 10.75"w. Fork and spoon, 7.38"long x 1.88"w. Backstamps: 58.0 (all items marked). Set, as shown, $250-300.

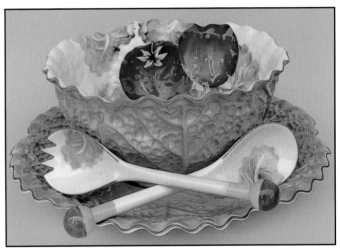

Salad bowl set (B.759). Bowl, 3.63"h x 8.0"w x 3.75"d. Fork and spoon, 7.25"long x 1.88"w. Plate, 1.25"h x 11.0"w. Backstamps: 54.0. Set, as shown, $180-280.

Salad bowl set (B.757). Bowl, 4.5"h x 8.13"w. Plate, 1.0"h x 10.63"w. Backstamps: 27.1 (plate unmarked). Set, as shown, $180-280.

Salad bowl set (B.760). Bowl, 4.63"h x 10.0"w x 8.25"d. Fork and spoon, 7.25"long x 1.88"d. Individual plates, .88"h x 7.5"dia. Backstamps: 25.1. Set, as shown, $180-280.

Cracker bowl (B.761). 2.5"h x 8.75"w x 3.5"d. Backstamp: 19.2. $40-80.

Mster snack serving bowl (B.763) Why? See B.768. 3.13"h x 6.0"w. Backstamp: 27.1. Item shown, $40-80.

Fruit drainer (B.762) Bowl, 2.13"h x 7.75"w. Plate, 1.13"h x 8.13"w. Backstamp: 54.0. $40-90.

Alternate view (B.763A) of B.763.

Alternate view (B.762A) f B.762.

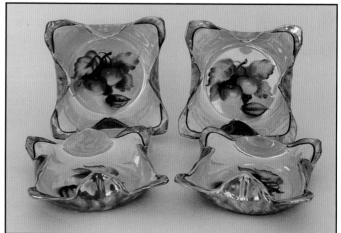

Individual snack bowls (B.764). These would go with a matching master bowl that, in terms of shape, would be like the one shown in B.767. 1.13"h x 3.5"w. Backstamps: 27.1. Each, $30-40.

Gravy (sauce) boat (part of a fish set) (B.765). 3.25"h x 8.88"w x 5.75"d. Backstamp: 27.1. $90-140.

Covered box (B.767). 7.0"h x 5.0"w x 4.0"d. Backstamp: 27.1. $4000+

Covered box (B.766). 9.5"h x 4.38"w x 4.0"d.
Backstamp: 27.1. $3000+

Covered box (B.767A) with matching trinket dish. The box is another example of B.767; it offers an alternate view. Trinket dish, 4.0"h x 5.0"w x 5.0"d. Backstamps: 27.1. Trinket dish, $800+

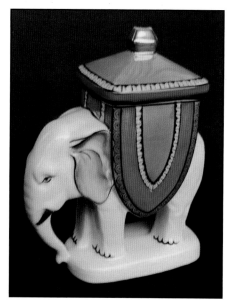

Covered box (B.768). The painted toes are an unusual feature. 6.38"h x 5.13"w x 2.75"d. Backstamp: 19.2. $900+

Covered box (B.769). 6.25"h x 5.0"w x 3.5"d. Backstamp: 27.0. $900+

Covered box (B.770). 5.5"h x 3.75"w. Backstamp: 16.0. $2000+

Alternate view (B.769A) of B.769.

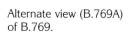

Detail (B.770A) of B.770.

Covered box (B.771). 5.25"h x 4.75"w. Backstamp: 16.0. $200+

Covered box (B.772). 4.25"h x 6.25"w. Backstamp: 16.0. $120-190.

Alternate view (B.772A) of B.772.

Covered box (B.773). 4.25"h x 6.63"w. Backstamp: 27.1. $120-190.

Covered box (B.774). 4.75"h x 6.88"w x 2.75"d. Backstamp: 27.1. $60-90.

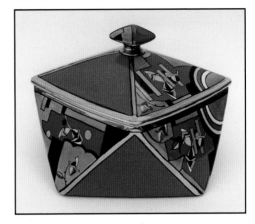

Covered box (B.775). 4.5"h x 6.0"w x 4.5"d. Backstamp: 16.0. $450+

Covered box (B.776). 2.88"h x 4.0"w. Backstamp: 27.0: $90-140.

Alternate view (B.776A) of B.776.

Condiment Sets and Related Items

All of the items shown in the photos of this chapter are thought by most collectors and dealers to have been intended, for the storing and/or serving of condiments—i.e., things one normally eats *with* food, not *as* food. Specifically, one will find:

Repeatedly, when fellow Noritake collectors show me their collection for the first time, they take me first to the display cabinet or book shelf where their most prized items are on display. And why not? They have worked hard to find those items and, often, have paid a great deal for them. And, truth be told, I do the same when people come to see my collection. Lady plates, dresser dolls and other figural lady items, items with Deco geometric motifs, powder puff boxes—these are the sorts of items that are likely to be in that imposing cabinet or on that special shelf. Few such displays, however, are likely to include mayonnaise sets and honey pots or jam jars and condiment sets.

And yet, as I have said in one way or another at the start of previous chapter Cs, I frequently find that condiment sets are among the most interesting and impressive of the Noritake items shown to me by collectors. After you have examined the items shown in the photos of this chapter, I think you will see what I mean.

There are risks, always, in saying that a particular item is the most important, rare or interesting one in a chapter. Opinions on such matters are subjective and it is almost certain that others will disagree and, sometimes, will feel slighted. Even so, I am about to discuss seven items shown in this chapter that in my opinion, are especially significant.

Moving from the start of the chapter toward the end, the first such exceptionally important item is the figural elephant condiment set shown in C.253. Very few complete examples are known (though as always, true collectors will hope at least a few others will be found), and it is easy to see why. We can imagine,

for example, how quickly and easily the lid of the mustard pot (the topmost piece) would be knocked off and broken. So this item is impressive just for being complete. It is also of interest, however, for another reason. The only backstamp is the word "Japan" (in red) and it is located on the bottom of the left front foot. To see it, the set must be taken apart. Fortunately, for Noritake collectors, the shape, size and color of the letters is exactly the same as that seen on known Noritake items. But, there is room on the bottoms of the salt and pepper shakers for a full backstamp. Since the piece is so imposing, it seems there would have been a desire to use the full backstamp if at all possible. Consequently, lingering doubts about the provenance of this piece remained in the minds of some. For two reasons, a solid shift in opinion on the matter has occurred in recent years. First, the quality of the porcelain seems well within what we have come to expect in Noritake fancyware from this period. Second, the unusual pearlized blue luster has been found on Noritake items with a full backstamp. Our confidence would be total, of course, with documentation from the Noritake Company itself or from the discovery of ads in magazines or trade journals that show the piece. One hopes that such materials will be found in the not too distant future.

One of the rarest and oddest items shown in this book can be seen in C.267. The design of this condiment set is very clever. In *this* condiment set, there is no way the mustard pot will fall off of the undertray. It is the only such set I have ever seen and, happily, it has a striking and well-executed motif.

Before discussing the next item, I would like to ask you, dear reader, to first look at photo C.280. Before reading the next sentence, turn to that photo and see if you know what is unusual about the item shown in it. [I will pause while you look. Are you back? OK, then we can continue.] Even experienced collectors may wonder what it is that is so unusual about that lovely jam set. Actually, there are at least two things that stand out. One of them is the way it is decorated. The white pearl luster glaze with the red trim and red apple is exceptionally well conceived, I think, and it is quite unusual (in this regard, also note the red trim on the matching spoon). For many, this alone would make the set worthy of some comment, and I would agree.

But this set has an even more distinctive feature: the underplate. During my more than 20 years of avid collecting and viewing of Noritake collections (dozens of them all over the continent and abroad), I have seen countless jam pots with the large apple finial. To the best of my recollection, however, not one of them had an underplate. Indeed, this trend was so pronounced I began to be convinced that, for some reason, "big apple" jam sets simply never came with underplates. For several reasons, however, that view seemed so odd, so unbelievable. In the first place, underplates were known to be part of every other kind of Noritake jam set I or anyone I knew had seen. Second, such plates are both functional as well as significant from an aesthetic standpoint. Even so, the facts from all those collections could not be denied. Therefore, when this set showed up in a nearby friend's collection, one of the first things I wanted to see was the *bottom* of the underplate. Was there a backstamp on it? If so, I would have said that it was not a true underplate because, *generally* (there are numerous exceptions, unfortunately) underplates on Noritake items do not have a backstamp. Significantly, there is no backstamp on the underplate with this set.

As often happens, however, when one mystery is resolved, another one appears. We now can say, confidently, that at least some big apple jam sets had underplates. But, did they all have them? If so, why is it that there are so few with the sets we see today? Breakage would be the immediate reply, of course, but that doesn't quite satisfy me. Is it not the case that we can reasonably expect breakage to be a problem of equal significance for all Noritake jam sets with underplates? If so, then why are there so few underplates for big apple jam sets and so many with other sets? And while we are on the subject of underplates, have a look at the item shown in C.293. Please look at it before reading the next paragraph.

Just as the jam set we just discussed, the sauce set shown in C.293 is unique, at least in my experience. And, once again, the way it is decorated is one aspect of this. No doubt there are many other examples of Noritake sauce sets where the rim of the bowl is decorated the way this one is but, so far, I have not seen another. What really should raise eyebrows, however and especially for the experienced collector, is the underplate. For all the world, it looks like a lemon plate, and a fairly uncommon one at that (only two have been shown so far in my books; see P.169 and P.170 in *Collecting Noritake A to Z*). What also struck me immediately, when I saw this set, was that the sauce bowl did not fit well on the underplate. The figural butterfly seems to be in the way. Although the bowl does not touch it when centered, the gap is extremely small. For these reasons, I doubted that it was a true set; instead, I guessed that it was a marriage—an interesting one but a marriage nonetheless. That initial thought, however, seems incorrect on two grounds. First and foremost, the underplate does not have a backstamp. Virtually every lemon plate that initially was sold alone as a lemon plate would have had a backstamp. We must say "virtually" because there are a *few* exceptions. Some Noritake items never had backstamps and not for lack of a spot big enough for one. An example is shown in V.12 of *Noritake Collectibles A to Z* (other identical examples of that potpourri with the full backstamp are known, by the way). Even so, it seems highly unlikely (but not impossible) that this underplate was an unmarked lemon plate that was married with a sauce set missing its true underplate. Why? Because the underplate in C.293 has rim detailing that matches that of the sauce set in color (but color only, and this is, I admit, a point that weakens the case a bit). Ultimately, however, what clinches it for me is the mathematical improbability of it all. How likely is it that (1) a rare figural butterfly lemon plate that (2) lacks a backstamp but (3) has a rim detail that matches the color of another piece exactly should even exist, let alone (4) that it should be found by somebody who had a sauce set with a missing underplate that it could be "married" with?

The figural salt and pepper shakers shown in C.302 are quite rare and for that reason alone deserve special comment. I am mentioning them here, however, because they are one of the few instances we know of so far of a motif on a Noritake item found in both figural and applied (painted on) form. I am indebted to Gary Kaufman for having noted the rarity of this with a case involving other items. The item with the figures in C.302 painted on is a salt and pepper set shown in C.77 of *Noritake Collectibles A to Z*. The very next item shown, in C.303, is also extremely rare. There are *many* Noritake "bridesmaid" figural salt and pepper shakers out there and, for many collectors, they are all rather desirable. Often, they are found on oval trays (e.g., C.18 and C.19 of *Noritake Collectibles A to Z*). I have no doubt about the authenticity of those (and many other such) sets. The set shown in C.303, however, is unique (so far). The same applies equally to the set shown in C.305.

The last of the items I wish to discuss, but by no means the least of them, is shown in C.319. It is of interest because of what the box tells us. The slots in the box tell us that a *complete* stacking salt and pepper set consists of the undertray, the open salt dish and the pepper shaker which *can* be stacked on it (in part, perhaps, to keep the salt dry in humid climates). In the introduction to the Chapter C of *Noritake Fancyware A to Z*, I discuss a similar set shown in C.184. That set consists of a tray, stacking salt and pepper *and* a matching mustard pot with a spoon. "Because of this set," I said (on p.145), "we must now wonder whether the small trays with pepper shaker and a matching (unstacked) open salt … are, in fact, incomplete versions of a set like the one shown in C.184." Well, with the box shown in C.319, we now know *for sure* that at least some sets like these that do not have mustard pots *are* complete sets. Moreover, it also can be suggested that in this configuration it was probably not expected that the salt and pepper would be stacked. But as with the puzzle discussed above, the insights from this very important box yield yet other mysteries. Were there larger complete sets that came in boxes with slots specifically for the items in C.319 *plus* a mustard pot, lid and spoon such as are seen in the set in C.184? Or were some mustard pots sold separately as an "optional extra"? Were sets that *we* refer to as stacking salt and pepper sets *really* meant to be stacked? To solve puzzles like these, we need more time *and* other boxes.

Dozens of other very fine items are shown in this chapter. You will be relieved to know, I suspect, that I do not discuss them here. I am, however, about to *mention* some of them: C.252 (rare and complete; striking motif), C.258 (complete; rare itself for such items), C.259 (unusual; from Australia), C.266 (very unusual undertray), C.274 (it is light brown and a green version is shown in C.200; since Noritake color schemes often came in three, what is the third color likely to be? I vote for blue.), C.283 (*very* striking decoration; rare), C.286 (what is the third color of this conceptual set likely to be? again, I vote for blue.), C.289 (beautifully made and decorated), C.291 (bizarre motif that many will find unattractive; I can say this without being rude to the owner because it is my piece), C.301 (very striking motif), C.306 (how aware were you that the Dutch Boy and Girl came in two sizes?), C.307 (*very* unusual and striking motif), C.308 (an unusual number of luster colors for one piece), C.309 (the green set is an uncommon color), C.312 (rare), C.313 (super cute), C.324 (such a large set is itself unusual; that it is complete is simply amazing), C.325 (elegance all over the place), C.327 and C.328 (two fine examples of conceptual sets involving the three key colors: green, blue and tan luster).

Berry set (C.248). Sugar, 7.0"h x 3.0"w. Creamer, 6.25"h x 3.63"w x 3.0"d. Backstamps: 27.1. Set, $80-150.

Berry sets (C.249). Sugar, 6.5"h x 2.5"w. Creamer, 5.75"h x 3.38"w. Backstamps: *Left*, MIJ.1; *right*, 27.1. Each set, $70-90.

Butter dish (C.250). 3.13"h x 6.5"w. Backstamp: 27.1. $30-70.

Butter dish (C.251). 3.0"h x 5.5"w. Backstamp: 16.2. Set, as shown, $40-80.

Alternate view (C.251A) of C.251.

Condiment set (C.252). Tray, 4.13"h x 8.63"w x 5.25"d. Preserve jar, 3.63"h x 3.2.5"w. Salt and pepper shakers, 2.0"h x 1.0"w. Butter tub, 2.75"h x 3.38"w. Backstamps: Shakers, J.1; all others, 19.1. $90-160.

Condiment set (C.253). 5.5"h x 4.2.5"w x 5.25"d. Backstamps: J.1. $750+

Condiment set (C.255). Tray, 1.38"h x 6.5"w x 2.38"d. Shakers, 1.38"h x 2.0"w 1.75"d. Mustard jar, 2.5"h x 1.75"w. Overall, 2.75"h. Backstamps: Tray, C22.0; shakers, J.0w (30040). Complete set, $90-160.

Condiment set (C.256). Tray, 1.13"h x 7.0"w 2.5"d. Large bird, 2.75"h x 3.25"w x 2.0"d. Shakers, 1.5"h x 2.0"w x 1.13"d. Backstamps: Tray, unmarked; all others, 27.1. Set, as shown, $180-280.

Condiment set (C.254). 3.5"h x 4.38"w. Backstamps: Backstamps: 27.1. Set, as shown, $350-450.

Condiment set (C.257). Tray, 1.13"h x 7.0"w 2.5"d. Large bird, 2.75"h x 3.25"w x 2.0"d. Shakers, 1.5"h x 2.0"w x 1.13"d. Backstamps: 27.0. Set, as shown, $180-280.

Condiment set (C.258). Tray, 1.25"h x 7.5"w x 3.0"d. Shakers, 2.5"h x 1.63"w. Center pot, 3.13"h x 2.25"w. Backstamps: 27.1 (tray is marked). $190-290.

Condiment set (C.261). Tray, 1.13"h x 6.88"w x 2.63"d. Shakers, 3.13"h x 1.5"w. Mustard jar, 3.13"h x 3.0"w. Overall, 3.25"h. Backstamps: Tray, unmarked; shakers, J.1; mustard jar, 27.1. Complete set, $90-160.

Condiment set (C.259). Tray, .63"h x 7.5"w x 3.13"d. Shakers, 2.38"h x 1.75"w x1.75"d. Mustard jar, 2.88"h x 1.75"w x 1.75"d. Overall, 3.0"h. Backstamps: 58.0. Complete set, $80-120.

Condiment set (C.262). Tray, 1.25"h x 7.38"w x 3.0"d. Shakers, 2.75"h x 1.25"w. Mustard, 2.5"h x 2.13"w. Backstamps: Shakers, J.1; other items, 27.1. Complete set, $90-170.

Condiment set (C.260). Tray, 1.13"h x 6.88"w x 2.63"d. Shakers, 3.13"h x 1.5"w. Mustard jar, 3.13"h x 3.0"w. Overall, 3.25"h. Backstamps: Tray, unmarked; shakers, J.1; mustard jar, 27.1. Complete set, $110-180.

Condiment set (C.263). Tray, .75"h x 7.0"w x 2.88"d. Shakers, 1.38"h x 1.38"w. Mustard jar, 2.38"h x 2.0"w. Backstamps: Shakers, MIJ.0; others, 27.0. Complete set, $70-110.

Condiment set (C.264). Tray, 3.5"h x 4.38"w. Shakers, 2.5"h x 1.63"w. Toothpick holder, 1.75"h x 1.25"w. Mustard, 3.0"h x 2.5"w x 1.63"d. Backstamps: Mustard and tray, 27.1; others MIJ.1. Complete set, as shown, $60-90.

Condiment set (C.265). Overall, 3.88"h x 4.38"w x 3.63"d. Backstamps: 27.1. Complete set, $60-90.

Condiment set (C.266). 2.88"h x 4.38"w x 2.75"d. Backstamps: 27.1. Complete set, $80-110.

Condiment set (C.267) with rare attached tray. Shakers, 2.0"h x 1.0"w. Mustard jar, 2.38"h x 3.88"w. Backstamps: Shakers, MIJ.0; mustard jar, 27.0. $120-180.

Condiment sets (C.268). 3.0"h x 5.5"w x 4.75"d. Backstamps: 27.0; Each complete set, $90-140.

Condiment set (C.269). Tray, 4.88"dia. Shakers, 2.6"h x 1.38"w. Mustard jar, 2.5"h x 2.25"w. Backstamps: 27.1. Complete set, $70-100.

Condiment set (C.270). Tray, 1.13"h x 4.25"w x 4.13"d. Shakers, 2.63"h x 1.0"w. Mustard jar, 2.25"h x 2.25"w x 1.63"d. Backstamps: Tray, 25.1; shakers, J.1; mustard pot, MIJ.1. Complete set, $90-140.

Honey pot (C.273). 4.38"h x 3. 5"w x 3.25"w. Backstamp: 27.1. Complete set, $200-280.

Condiment set (C.271). 1.88"h x 3.0"w x 3.0"d. Backstamps: Tray and mustard, 27.0, shakers, J.0. Complete set, $40-80.

Honey pot (C.272). 3.75"h x 3.38"w. Backstamp: 27.1. Complete set, $180-270.

Jam set (C.274). Jam basket, 5.5"h x 3.75"w. Underplate, .88"h x 5.38"w. Backstamp (basket only): 27.0. Complete set, $350-450.

Jam jar (C.275) with attached underplate. 4.88"h x 4.75"w. Backstamp: 27.1. Complete set, $190-290.

Detail (C.275A) of C.275.

Jam set (C.276) with attached underplate and metal handle. 4.25"h x 5.38"w. With handle up, 6.0"h. Backstamp: 27.1. $80-150.

Jam set (C.277). 4.63"h x 7.88"w x 6.5"d. Backstamps: 19.1. Complete set, $70-100

Jam set (C.278). 5.25"h x 5.38"w. Backstamps: 27.1. Complete set, $40-60.

Jam sets (C.279). 5.13"h x 4.25"w. Backstamps: *Left,* 27.1; *right,* 31.7. Each complete set, $90-120.

Jam set (C.280). 5.38"h x 5.5"w. Backstamps: 27.1; underplate unmarked. Set, as shown, $90-130.

Jam set (C.283). 4.5"h x 5.5"w. Backstamps: spoon and jar, 27.0; underplate unmarked. Set, as shown, $80-130.

Jam set (C.281). 5.13"h x 5.5"w. Backstamps: 27.1; underplate unmarked. Complete set, $90-130.

Jam set (C.284). 4.25"h x 5.0"dia. Backstamps: spoon and jar, 27.0; underplate unmarked. Set, as shown, $80-130.

Jam set (C.282). 5.0"h x 5.5"w. Backstamps: 14.0. $80-110.

Jam set (C.285). 4.25"h x 5.0"w. Backstamps: 27.0. Set, as shown, $40-90.

Jam sets (C.286). 5.25"h x 6.5"w x 5.63"d. Backstamps: 25.1; underplates unmarked. Each set, $40-90.

Sauce sets (C.289). 2.5"h x 6.5"w. Backstamps: *Left,* 54.0; *right,* 25.1. Each set, $60-100.

Jam set (C.287). 5.0"h x 5.75"w. Backstamps: 27.0. Set, as shown, $40-80.

Mayonnaise set (C.290). 3.5"h x 6.25"w. Backstamps: 27.0. Set, $60-90.

Sauce set (C.288). 3.0"h x 6.25"w x 5.75"d. Backstamps: 27.1. Set, as shown, $30-50.

Mayonnaise set (C.291). 3.13"h x 5.38"w. Backstamps: 27.0. Set, $90-130.

Mayonnaise set (C.292). 3.13"h x 5.38"w. Backstamps: 27.0. Set, $70-100.

Mayonnaise set (C.295). Bowl, 2.5"h x 4.75"dia. Plate, 6.0"dia. Backstamps: 27.0. Set, $30-70.

Sauce set (C.293). Bowl, 1.88"h x 5.0"w. plate, 1.38"h x 6.0"w. Backstamps: Bowl, 27.1; underplate unmarked. Set, $90-130.

Mayonnaise set (C.296). 2.75"h x 5.88"w. Backstamps: 27.0; underplate unmarked. Set, $70-100.

Sauce set (C.294). 2.38"h x 5.38"w. Backstamps: 27.0. Set, $70-100.

Mayonnaise set (C.297). 2.75"h x 5.88"w. Backstamps: 27.1; underplate unmarked. Set, $80-130.

Mayonnaise set (C. 298). 2.25"h x 6.0"w.
Backstamps: 27.1. Set, $60-110.

Mustard pot (C. 299) with attached underplate.
3.38"h x 4.0"w. Backstamp: 27.0. Complete
with matching spoon, $50-80.

Oil and vinegar salad dressing set (C.300). 5.0"h x 8.5"w x
5.13"d. Backstamps: 27.1. Set, $140-180.

Oil and vinegar set (C.301). 3.75"h x 5.63"w x 2.75"d.
Backstamps: 25.1. Set, $120-180.

Salt and pepper set (C.302). *Left*, 3.63"h x
1.38"w x 1.13"d; *right*, 3.75"h x 1.38"w x
1.0"d. Backstamps: J.1. Pair, as shown,
$250+

Salt and pepper set (C.303) with rare matching tray. 3.63"h x
4.63"w x 2.0"d. Backstamps: Tray, 29.1; shakers, J.1. Set, as
shown, $270-370.

Salt and pepper set (C.304). 4.0"h x 1.5"w.
Backstamps: J.2. Pair, as shown, $160-210.

Salt and pepper set (C.307). Boy, 3.13"h x 1.25"w.
Girl, 3.25"h x 1.25"w. Backstamps: J.1. Pair, as
shown $240-340.

Salt and pepper set (C.305) with rare matching tray. 3.5"h
x 4.0"w x 1.75d. Backstamps: Tray, 27.1; salt and pepper,
J.1. Set, as shown, $260-360.

Salt and pepper set (C.308). 3.63"h x 1.5"w x
1.38"d. Backstamps: MIJ.1. Pair, as shown,
$170-220.

Salt and pepper sets (C.306). *Left*, Boy, 3.75"h x 1.75"w. Girl,
4.0"h x 1.75"w. *Right*, Boy, 3.13"h x 1.25"w. Girl, 3.25"h x 1.25"w.
Backstamps: J.1. Each pair, $180-280.

Salt and pepper sets (C.309). 3.38"h x 2.25"w x 2.0"d.
Backstamps: MIJ.1. Each pair, $150-200.

Salt and pepper sets (C.310). Blue set, 2.5"h x 1.25"w; red and yellow set, 2.0"h x 1.13"w; tan and blue set, 2.13"h x 1.0"w; blue and yellow set, 2.0"h x 1.13"w. Backstamps: Blue set, MIJ.1; others J.0. Each set, $90-160.

Salt and pepper set (C.313). 2.25"h x 2.0"w. Backstamps: MIJ.1. Pair, $160-220.

Salt and pepper set (C.311). 1.75"h x 1.38"w. Backstamps: J.1. Pair, $160-220.

Salt and pepper set (C.314). Pepper chicken, 1.63"h x 2.13"w x 1.5"d. Salt nest, 1.0"h x 2.5"w x 1.75"d. Backstamps: 27.0. Set, as shown, $70-120.

Salt and pepper set (C.312). 2.63"h x 4.63"w x 1.0"d. Backstamps: J.1. Pair, $150-200.

Alternate view (C.314A) of C.314.

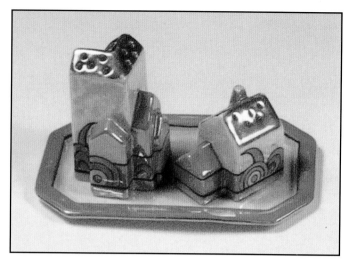

Salt and pepper set (C.315). 2.5"h x 4.25"w. Backstamps: Tray, 27.1; salt and pepper shakers, MIJ.1. Set as shown, with uncommon matching tray, $170-220.

Salt and pepper set (C.318). Tray, 4.38"w x 2.63"d. Pepper, 2.63"h x 1.25"d. Backstamps: 27.1. $100-130.

Salt and pepper set (C.316). 2.0"h x 4.38"w x 2.63"d. Backstamps: Tray, 27.1; open salt, MIJ.1; bird pepper, J.1. $140-190.

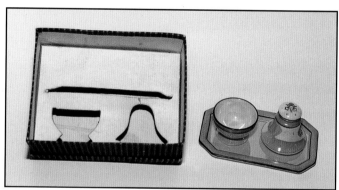

Salt and pepper set (C.319) with original box. The box shows that this set, at least, was complete without a spoon or a mustard pot. Tray, 4.38"w x 2.63"d. Open salt, 1.0"h x 1.63"w. Pepper, 1.75"h x 1.75"w. Box (with sticker that reads: 2675/24, 1 Set, Made in Japan), 2.5"h x 5.25"w x 3.75"d. Backstamps: Open salt, MIJ.0; pepper, J.0; tray, unmarked. Set with box, as shown, $130-180.

Salt and pepper set (C.317). Tray, 4.38"w x 2.63"d. Pepper, 2.25"h. Backstamps: 27.0. $100-130.

Salt and pepper sets (C.320). *Left*, 4.75"h x 1.63"w; *right*, 4.75"h x 1.5"w. Backstamps, MIJ.1. Each set, $40-80.

Salt and pepper set (C.321). 4.75"h x 1.5"w. Backstamps: MIJ.1. Pair, $40-80.

Salt and pepper set (C.322), with original box. A note on the box indicates this was a wedding shower gift in 1928. Shakers, 3.0"h x 1.5"w. Box, 1.75"h x 3.5"w x 3.5"d. Backstamps: MIJ.1w. Set, as shown, $60-100.

Salt and pepper set (C.323), arranged to show front and back. 2.38"h x 2.5"w x 2.13"d. Backstamps: 27.0. Pair, $40-60.

Salt and pepper sets (C.324) in caddy. Overall, 3.75"h x 5.38"w; individual shaker, 1.75"h x 1.5"w. Backstamps: 27.1. Complete set, $100-150.

Open salts (C.325). 2.5"h x 3.0"w x 2.13"d. Backstamps: 25.1. Each, $80-110.

Open salts (C.326) in original box. Swans, 1.63"h x 2.38"w x 1.63"d. Box, 1.75"h x 5.38"w x 5.38"d. Backstamps: 27.1. Set, as shown, $150-250.

Syrup set (C.329). 4.63"h x 5.5"w. Backstamp: 27.0. Set, $40-70.

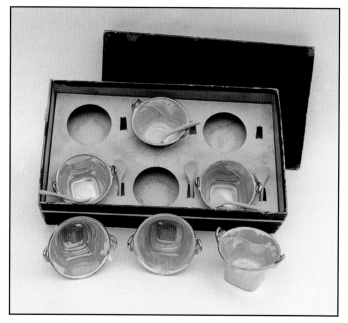

Open salts (C.327), with wooden spoons, in original box. Salts, 1.25"h x 2.13"w x 1.88"d. Box, 1.63"h x 7.75"w x 1.88"d. Backstamps: 27.0. Set, as shown, $100-150.

Open salts (C.328). .75"h x 2.0"w. Backstamps: 27.0. Set, as shown, $150-200.

Syrup set (C.330). 4.25"h x 5.5"w. Backstamp: Pitcher, 19.0; underplate, unmarked. Set, $40-70.

Chapter D
Desk and Dresser Items

In this chapter, one will find photos of the following kinds of items meant for use on and around desks and dressers:

Desk items
Desk sets (p.124)
Inkwells (pp.124-125)

Dresser items
Dresser dolls (pp.125-126)
Dresser sets (p.127)
Dresser trays (pp.127-128)
Hat pin holder (p.128)
Perfume bottles (pp.128-129)
Pin trays (pp.129-130)
Powder boxes and jars (pp.131-133)
Powder puff boxes (pp.133-135)
Talcum powder shakers (p.135)
Trinket boxes, dishes and trays (pp.135-136)

When an after-dinner speaker is truly famous, the introduction often is quite brief. Sufficient would be some version of "We have with us here tonight a person who genuinely needs no introduction." Although there are exceptions (at our national political conventions, for example), the general rule seems to be that the length of an introduction is related inversely to the speaker's reputation or fame. If a comparable rule is applied to this book, the introduction to Chapter D should certainly be the shortest of all (and by a wide margin). Among Noritake collectors and dealers, there simply is no other general type of Noritake fancyware that is more famous, admired or sought-after than the type presented in this chapter. Compared to other categories of Noritake fancyware, a very high portion of the "desk and dresser" items have features that most collectors are looking for: figural shapes (and especially lady figurals) and Deco motifs including, especially, Deco ladies as well as Deco geometrics and florals. The value figures in this chapter reflect this fact.

Although the temptation to do more is great, I offer a few brief remarks about roughly a dozen pieces. The first two items shown in this chapter (D.210 and D.211) can be thought of as relatively rare simply because each has all three lids. They are shown here as "desk sets" but there continues to be some discussion among collectors as to whether this fairly commonly heard designation is correct. Some hold that these items were used not for pen nibs, paper clips, stamps and the like but, rather, for powders, eyeliner pencils, rouge and other cosmetic items. Since I have no information that will settle this, I can do no more than alert the reader to the fact of this ongoing discussion.

I would draw your attention now to two dresser sets which, taken together, constitute a truly stunning display. The first of these, D.219, is one of the most remarkable Noritake Deco dresser sets I have ever seen (disclosure: neither this nor the next set is mine; sigh…). The motif is superb, the set is large and last, but hardly least, it is complete. Besides its basic attractiveness, the second one, in D.220, is most notable for its tray. Until this one, which I saw rather recently, I had not known of a dresser tray in this shape. Since large heart-shaped dresser trays are known, must we now be on the lookout for spade and diamond shaped trays of approximately this size? The very next item, the tray shown in D.221, is generally regarded as one of the most dramatic Deco lady motifs known to Noritake collectors.

Any example of a two-piece figural lady perfume bottle of the type shown in D.230 would be comment-worthy, but the decoration on this one makes it all the more deserving. The piece is both rare and has a particularly attractive, well-executed motif. The same points apply to the figural lady powder box shown in D.238. Boxes like this are relatively rare and, one suspects, the motif on this particular example will be new for and rather appealing to many. One of the rarest items shown in this book is the figural lady powder box shown in D.239. We know that this *magnificent* two-piece box came in other colors because collectors have seen a distinctive bottom or two. As of now, however, this is the only complete example that I know of (once again, I feel I should emphasize that it is not mine).

As has been the case for at least 20 years, powder puff boxes with Deco lady motifs are very popular with Noritake collectors. The one shown in D.254 is not only beautifully designed but also quite rare (at least so far). The very next photo (D.255) shows another rather infrequently seen puff box that is very different in its general tone, although no less desirable for the fact (at least to most powder puff box fanciers). Obviously, it is not possible for every Noritake item to be spectacular. Fortunately, however, our interest in even relatively modest items is likely to increase when they are grouped with several other very similar ones (indeed, this very likely is at least part of the appeal of collecting itself). In this book, there are several photographs that illustrate this; in this chapter, the best example is D.258, which shows five non-figural talcum powder shakers that, together, make a *very* satisfying display (individually they are nice, too).

For several reasons, the next-to-last last item to be mentioned is one of the more surprising pieces shown in the book. I refer to the heart-shaped trinket box in D.260. Although such trinket boxes are hardly common, they are a fairly well known type of dresser item. Similarly, the "lady in yellow bonnet" motif that is on the one shown in D.260 is also reasonably well known although it hardly could be called common (the motif appears on the powder puff box shown in D.146, p.105 of *Collecting Noritake A to Z*). On this trinket box, however, the lady has a dark red dress, not the light orange seen on the more familiar examples. And the image on this box is oriented so that the lady's hat is near the point of the heart—i.e., just the opposite of the way the motifs are arranged on the other heart-shaped trinket boxes I know of (two are shown in this book; see D.261). Significantly, this Noritake box was not made for export; it was intended for the domestic (Japanese) market and, as it happens, it is part of a Noritake collection in Japan.

Finally, I direct your attention to the last photo of the chapter (D.265). Both of the items shown in it are *extremely* rare and quite elegant; they deserve discussion on those counts alone. I, however, need to discuss them with reference to their function. They are listed as "trinket dishes," which seems plausible given their general shape. But are they really? Of course (and if you stop to really think about it), the answer cannot be "no" (at least not with certainty) because if I knew for sure that "no" was the answer, the photo probably would have been shown in another chapter. Evidently, therefore, it is at least possible that they are indeed trinket dishes. But, for reasons to be noted, I think it is just as likely that they are ashtrays. I did not put the photo of them in Chapter A, however, because neither item has a groove in which to place a cigarette when the item is being used as an ashtray—a required feature if they are to meet my (admittedly stringent) definition of an ashtray.

But why, then, do I raise any question about the function of these pieces? Because the figural portions of these items match quite precisely a famous figural item: the covered box known to most collectors as the "Seated Lady." In this book, a truly extraordinary example is shown near the end of Chapter B; indeed, in one of those photos (B.767A), the covered box and one of these "trinket dishes" are shown together. In the captions for similar covered boxes shown in my first two books, I noted that at least one highly regarded publication states that the Seated Lady is a cigarette box. For two reasons, this claim has always seemed plausible to me. First, the size of the inside of the box is such that it could hold cigarettes of the sort available in the 1920s. Second and more important in my view, the lady sitting in the chair is depicted as holding a cigarette. As you will recall, this detail is the standard way to differentiate certain fairly slim "dresser dolls" (e.g., D.217) from somewhat similar figural lady "cigarette jars" (e.g., A.254). If the Seated Lady is in fact a cigarette box it then becomes far more plausible to say that the "trinket dishes" in D.265 that clearly are mates to those boxes must be ashtrays. If all this is so, then why have I not put the photos of the Seated Lady and the figural lady "trinket dishes" in Chapter A? There are two reasons. First, it is not firmly established that the items are smoking related. Second, those familiar with my previous books and the principles used to place photos of various kinds of items will expect that Seated Lady boxes will be shown in the Bowls and Boxes chapter, and that few if any potential ashtrays that lack cigarette rests will be shown in Chapter A.

Inkwell (D.212). 4.25"h x 2.63"w. Backstamp: 27.1. $1000+

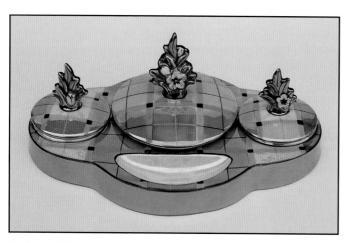

Desk set (D.210). 3.13"h x 8.5"w x 5.5"d. Backstamp: 27.1. $350-550

Desk set (D.211). 3.13"h x 8.5"w x 5.5"d. Backstamp: 27.1. $350-550.

Alternate view (D.212A) of D.212.

124

Desk/dresser box (*left*) and ink well (*right*) (D.213). Desk/dresser box, 4.75"h x 3.5"w. Inkwell, 4.5"h x 2.25"w. Backstamps: 27.1. *Left*, $200-300; *right* $140-210.

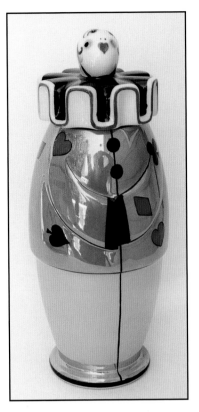

Dresser doll (D.215). 8.75"h x 3.5"w. Backstamp: 27.1. $1500-2000.

Ink well (D.214). 3.13"h x 2.25"w. Backstamp: 27.1. $180-280.

Alternate view (D.215A) of the lid in D.215.

Dresser doll (D.216). 6.0"h x 3.5"w. Backstamp: 29.0. $900-1400.

Alternate view (D.214A) of D.214.

Dresser doll (D.217). 6.0"h x 3.5"w. Backstamp: 29.0 (25920). $900-1400.

Dresser doll (D.218). 4.5"h x 1.75"w. Backstamp: 27.1. $200-400.

Detail (D.217A) of D.217.

Detail (D.218A) of D.218.

Dresser set (D.219). Tray, .63"h x 10.25"w x 7.0"d. Covered jar, 2.0"h x 2.63"w. Vase, 4.5"h x 2.13"w. Pin dish, 1.25"h x 3.0"w. Powder jar, 5.63"h x 3.5"w. Backstamp: 16.0. Set as shown, $2500+

Alternate view (D.219A) of the tray in D.219.

Dresser tray (D.221). .75"h x 11.0"w x 6.0"d. Backstamp: 27.1. $1800+

Dresser set (D.220). Tray, .5"h x 8.38"w x 8.25"d. Powder puff box, .75"h x 3.38"w. Perfume, 4.0"h x 2.63"w x 1.25"d. Backstamp: 27.1. Set, as shown, $800+

Detail (D.221A) of D.221.

Dresser tray (D.222). .38"h x 8.5"w x 5.75"d. Backstamp: 27.1. $600-800.

Perfume bottle (D.224). 4.75"h x 3.5"w. Backstamp: 19.0. $50-90.

Detail (D.222A) of D.222.

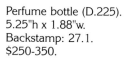

Perfume bottle (D.225). 5.25"h x 1.88"w. Backstamp: 27.1. $250-350.

Perfume bottle (D.226). 5.25"h x 1.88"w. Backstamp: 27.1. $200-300.

Hatpin holder (D.223). 4.75"h x 3.0"w. Backstamp: 19.0. $30-50

Perfume bottle (D.227). 6.0"h x 1.75"w. Backstamp: 27.1. $230-300.

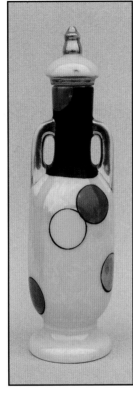

Perfume bottle (D.228). 6.0"h x 1.63"w. Backstamp: 27.1. $230-300.

Perfume bottle (D.230). 5.25"h x 2.25"w. Backstamp: 27.1. $600-750.

Alternate view (D.230A) of D.230. Dauber, 3.63" long.

Perfume bottles (D.229). 5.5"h x 2.5"w x 1.25"d. Backstamp: 27.1 on items with this motif, typically; these, however, are unmarked. Each, $250-350.

Pin tray (D.231). 1.63"h x 3.5"w. Backstamp: 16.2. $80-130.

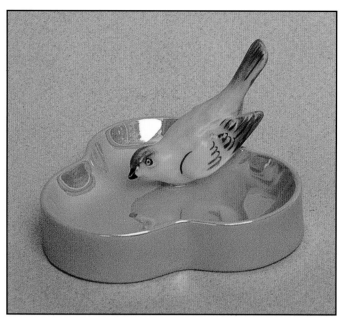

Pin tray (D.232). 2.25"h x 3.5"w. Backstamp: 27.0. $80-130.

Pin trays (D.235). 1.63"h x 1.78"w. Backstamps: 27.1. Each, $110-190.

Pin trays (D.233). *Left,* 2.0"h x 3.5"w. *Right,* 1.63"h x 3.75"w. Backstamps: 27.0. Each, $80-130.

Pin trays (D.236). 2.13"h x 2.75"w. Backstamps: *Right,* 26.0; *others,* 27.0. Each, $100-180.

Pin tray (D.234). 2.0"h x 2.63"w. Backstamp: 07.0. $150-200.

Pin tray (D.237). .5"h x 5.13"w x 3.88"d. Backstamp: 27.1. $180-230.

Powder box (D.238). 6.5"h x 6.25"w. Backstamp: 29.0 (25920).
$3000+

Powder box (D.240). 4.88"h x 5.63"w. Backstamp: 19.0. $600-800.

Powder box (D.239). 6.25"h x 8.5" x 3.75"w. Backstamp: 27.1.
$3300+

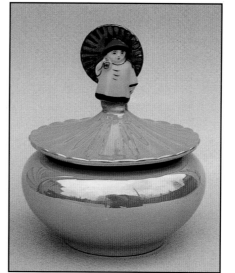

Powder box (D.241).
5.88"h x 4.88"w.
Backstamp: 27.0.
$600-800.

Detail (D.241A) of D.241.

Powder box (D.242). 5.5"h x 4.0"w. Backstamp: 29.0 (25920). $1000-1400.

Powder box (D.243). 5.63"h x 3.25"w. Backstamp: 29.1 (25920). $1000-1400.

Detail (D.242A) of D.242.

Powder box (D.244). 4.0"h x 4.0"w. Backstamp: 19.2. $220-320.

Powder box (D.245). 2.88"h x 6.0"w x 4.5"d.
Backstamp: 25.1. $90-170.

Powder puff box (D.248). 1.0 "h x 4.0"dia.
Backstamp: 27.1. $200-250.

Powder puff box (D.246). 3.5"h x 3.88"dia.
Backstamp: 29.1. $190-240.

Powder puff box (D.249). 1.0"h x 3.75"dia.
Backstamp: 27.1. $150-200.

Powder puff box (D.247). 1.75"h x 4.25"dia. Backstamp: 26.0.
$180-230.

Powder puff box (D.250). 1.5"h x 4.0"dia.
Backstamp: 27.1. $180-230.

Powder puff box (D.251). 1.5"h x 4.0"dia.
Backstamp: 27.1 $180-230.

Powder puff box (D.254). .75"h x 3.75"dia. Backstamp:
27.1. $500-750.

Powder puff box (D.252). 1.25"h x 4.75"w.
Backstamp: 27.1. $170-220.

Powder puff box (D.255). .75"h x 3.25"dia.
Backstamp: 27.1. $350-500.

Powder puff box (D.253). 1.0"h x 4.0"dia. Backstamp:
27.1. $250-300.

Powder puff box (D.256). .75"h x 3.63"dia.
Backstamp: 27.1. $250-400.

Talcum shaker (D.259).
6.0"h x 2.5"w. Backstamp:
MIJ.1. $300-450.

Powder puff box (D.257). 1.25"h x 3.63"dia. Backstamp: 27.1.
$130-170.

Trinket box (D.260). 1.25"h x 3.63"w. Backstamp: RC26.2. $500+

Talcum shakers (D.258). 6.25"h x 2.88"w. Backstamps: *From left to right*, MIJ.1, MIJ.0, 27.0, 27.0, MIJ.0. Each, $150-200, except second from left, $250-350.

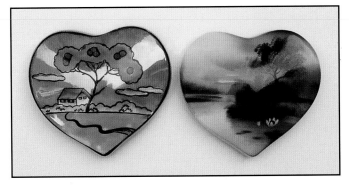

Trinket boxes (D.261). 1.25"h x 3.63"w. Backstamps: *Left*, 19.0; *right*, 27.1. *Left*, $200-300; *right*, $80-150.

Detail (D.262A)
of D.262.

Trinket trays (D.264). 1.0"h x 5.38"w x 5.0"d. Backstamps: 25.1.
Each, $40-90.

Trinket dish (D.262). 4.25"h x 5.0"w x 5.0"d.
Backstamp: 27.0. $450-750.

Trinket dish (D.263).
3.5"h x 5.0"w.
Backstamp: 27.1.
$850-1250.

Detail (D.263A)
of D.263.

Trinket dishes (D.265). 4.0 "h x 5.0"w x 5.0"d. Backstamps: 27.1.
Each, $800+

Chapter E
Ephemera Pertaining to
Noritake Fancyware Designs

In the 1920s, as in the decade before, the modest-sized Morimura Bros. (Noritake) design studio in New York had a *huge* task: to develop literally thousands of different market-worthy designs in a short time. One way to ease the burden, one can imagine, is to borrow ideas, an apparently time-honored approach in the world of ceramics design (the case of "Blue Willow" being one of the best known). In recent years, Noritake collectors have begun actively to search for possible design sources. Hints of this can be seen in *Noritake Collectibles A to Z* (pp.14-15). A more extended discussion of the matter is in the Chapter E in *Noritake Fancyware A to Z* (pp.184-192). In that chapter, the emphasis was on design themes and images that clearly correspond quite closely to images found on contemporary contract bridge ephemera (bridge tallies, score sheets, playing cards and the like), but other paper ephemera also were shown and discussed (a print by Marygold, for example).

This Chapter E also has a focus: pochoir prints that correspond to designs on Noritake fancyware (for assistance with the preparation of this chapter, I wish to thank Margaret Hetzler and, especially, Lita Kaufman). "Pochoir" is the French word for "stencil." Pochoir prints are made using stencils, typically a different one being cut for each color. The technique was utilized extensively by the publishers of French fashion magazines especially during the first two decades of the 20th century. Consequently, French artists and artisans created many of the currrently famous pochoir art works. Although there were several very famous pochoir artists who hailed from other parts of Europe, they too worked in France for the most part. Interestingly, given that the materials in this book were made in Japan, the pochoir method began rapidly to increase in popularity after French artists discovered similar Japanese printmaking techniques in the late 19th century. This development is but one of many that can be traced to the "Japan craze" ("Japonnisme") as it was lived out in France (the American version of the craze is discussed above in Chapter 2). The peak period for pochoir prints, however, was the 1920s.

The term "pochoir" is used to refer both to the technique or process and to the result—the pochoir print. Typically, these prints were produced by an artist plus a team of skilled artisans. The complete process involved five steps. First, an artist painted the master image. The team of artisans would then closely analyze the image in order to identify each and every color in it. Third, the team would cut separate stencils for each color from either oiled paper, in the early days or, later on, thin zinc or copper sheets. Fourth, the artisans would apply paint (gouache, predominantly; watercolor at times in the early years) to the appropri-

ate paper stock one stencil at a time. Depending upon the look that was desired, brushes of varying size and character would be used. Sponges or other paint-carrying devices also were used to fill in the spaces defined by the various stencils which, of course, had to be aligned perfectly to achieve the desired results. The last step, removing the stencil, may seem too obvious to warrant mention but it was in fact one of the more delicate maneuvers in the whole process.

For collectors and others interested in pochoir prints from the early 20th century, 4 or 5 artists seem always to command special regard for being the most skillful, prolific and influential of the many individuals working in this field. In alphabetical order, they are George Barbier (1882-1932), Pierre Brissaud (1885-1964), Umberto Brunelleschi (1879-1949), George Lepape (1887-1971) and André Marty (1882-1974). Of these, the works of Brunelleschi are of special significance for collectors of 1920s Noritake fancyware. His illustrations often were inspired by the figures of the Comedia del Arte, the masking traditions of Venice and especially the vogue for fancy dress balls featuring 18th century costumes. The images on the Noritake items shown in photo P.175 of *Collecting Noritake* and in P.87 and P.136 of *Noritake Collectibles* seem almost surely to have been inspired by Brunelleschi works or, perhaps, by works created by other pochoir artists who were influenced by Brunelleschi (for example, Max Ninon).

A far more clear-cut example of a Noritake item with a motif that can be linked to a Brunelleschi pochoir print is the tray shown in E.21 (the tray also is shown on p.233 of *Noritake Collectibles*, P.134 and P.134A). With just a glance at this Brunelleschi print, known as "The Fisherman," there can be no doubt that it and the tray motifs are linked. At 5.0" high, the tray is only a little smaller than the print, but what the print lacks in size it easily makes up for in quality.

Pochoir print by Brunelleschi with a Noritake tray with a corresponding motif (E.21). Print, 5.5"h x 5.5"w. Tray, 1.0"h x 10.0"w x 5.0"d. Backstamp: 27.1. $400+

Little is known about some of the artists who produced the pochoir prints in the 1920s. An example of importance to Noritake collectors is an Italian artist who signed his (or her; many pochoir artists used several names and there seems to be some uncertainty about this person's gender, although most references do use masculine pronouns when referring to this artist) works as "Leone M". One of the most frequently seen of the many so-called "lady motifs" on Noritake fancyware is one that many collectors refer to as the "Plantation Lady" (or sometimes "Southern Belle"). Tea sets, berry sets, trays, plates of various types and sizes, bowls and other Noritake items featuring this motif are known. As it happens, there is a pochoir print signed "Leone M" with the main features of that Noritake motif, though the lady is looking in the opposite direction. It also lacks certain features—most notably the male supplicant (see photos E.22-E.22B). Another print by "Leone M" (see E.23-E.23B) also has a clear link to a motif found on Noritake fancyware items and in this instance also, the image of the woman is reversed and the men have been deleted.

E.22 Pochoir signed by "Leone M" and a Noritake plate with a corresponding motif (E.22). Print, overall, 14.0"h x 17.0"w. Image, 10.5"h x 13.75"w. Plate, 1.13"h x 8.63"dia. Backstamp: 27.1. $350-450.

Detail (E.22A) of print in E.22.

Detail (E.22B) of plate in E.22.

Pochoir print signed by "Leone M" (E.23). Print, overall, 14.0"h x 17.0"w. Image, 10.25"h x 13.75"w.

Noritake plate (E.23B) that corresponds to the pochoir shown in E.23. Plate, 1.13"h x 8.63"dia. Backstamp: 27.1. $350-450.

Detail (E.23A) of E.23.

The New York design studio made good use of the ideas in two other pochoir prints also (see E.24-E.24B). Both are clearly related to two frequently seen Noritake fancyware motifs (see E.25-E.26). Interestingly, the studio made "editorial comments" that are similar to the ones made with the two previous examples—i.e., the men were deleted.

From the standpoint of dating these prints, it is informative to consider two more Leone pochoir prints that Ercoli, on p.169 of his important book *Art Deco Prints* (see *Bibliography*), dates as being from "c. 1925." Both of these prints exhibit general stylistic characteristics that are rather similar to the Leone prints discussed previously. Ercoli, however, also provides the names of these prints. The first one (E.27-E.27A) is "Riluttanza"; the second (E.28-E.28A) is "Adorazione." Indulging our fantasies, we may lament a little bit: would that the New York studio had sent designs based on these prints to Nagoya. What terrific items they would surely have been. So why weren't they used?

Two pochoir prints (E.24). Images, 9.13"h x 4.63"w.

Noritake motif (E.25) that corresponds with the pochoir print on the left in E.24.

Detail (E.24A) of print on the left in E.24.

Noritake motif (E.26) that corresponds with the pochoir print on the right in E.24.

Detail (E.24B) of print on the right in E.24.

"Riluttanza" - Pochoir print by Leone (E.27). Print image, including border, 11.38"h x 22.0"w.

"Adorazione" - Pochoir print by Leone (E.28). Print image, including border, 11.25"h x 22.0"w.

Detail (E.27A) of E.27.

Detail (E.28A) of E.28.

Chapter F
Figurines

Twenty-five excellent Noritake backstamped figurines are shown in this chapter. They are grouped by their basic forms; these are sequenced alphabetically as shown below.

Birds (pp.142-143)
Dragon (p.143)
Fish (p.143)
Humans (pp.143-144)
Mammals (pp.144-145)

All of the figurines shown here are unusual in one way or another and deserve comment but I limit my discussion to four items that are especially noteworthy. I begin with the Geisha figurine shown in F.54. This item is rarely seen in North America in large part, I suspect, because it originally was exported to Australia but also, one can wager, because current owners of them are reluctant to let them go. An American collector purchased this one on the Internet.

The figurine of the Japanese girl in F.59 appears to be the playmate (sibling?) of the boy shown in F.27 in *Collecting Noritake A to Z* (p.110). That the figure in the earlier photo definitely is a boy is established in part by the off-the-shoulder robe; a Japanese girl, I am told, would not wear her robe that way. Curiously, though, the boy is holding a "Temari"—a traditional ball made of elaborately woven colored thread, something that is usually played with by girls. (For more information on Temari balls, do a Google search and/or check your library for one of the books on the subject by Diana Vandervoort; see *Bibliography*, below, for a reference to one of them.) This puzzling combination starts to make more sense when it is noticed that the girl in F.59 is holding a toy that boys would typically

use. Are they siblings fighting over these toys, or are they giving them to each other as gifts? As I look at their faces and posture, I sense that it is the latter, but it is only a guess.

As it happens, the next photo (F.60) also shows a figurine that is a mate to a previously shown item: F.43 on p.197 of *Noritake Fancyware A to Z*. The bust of Arnold Palmer shown in F.60 was an edition of 300; the full figure showing Mr. Palmer putting (F.43) was an edition of 600. Mr. Palmer visited the Noritake Company in Nagoya on April 26, 1974. In that year, the Noritake Company produced several figurines and other items linked to Mr. Palmer. These items became available in the Unite States in 1975.

The figurines shown in F.62 and F.63 are a first for my books on Noritake. These wonderfully whimsical animals were designed for the Noritake Company by Mr. Kiyotada Itoh, Professor of Art Design at Tokyo Liberal Arts University. In 1978, five figurines were produced in this series: the sheep and musk ox that are shown here as well as a rhinoceros, lion and hippopotamus. Except for the sheep and lion, those meant for export were chocolate brown in color. Some dark green versions were made for the domestic market. Although not porcelain (unlike the other pieces shown in this book), these delightful pieces are becoming increasingly popular with collectors, and for good reason: every one you see brings a happy smile to your face.

Figurines (F.49). Sitting, 3.63"h x 4.0"w x 9.13"d. Standing, 6.63"h x 4.38"w x 6.0"d. Backstamps: *Left,* 67.019; *right,* 65.5. *Left,* $150-200; *right,* $180-280.

Figurines (F.50). Male, 10.5"h x 3.0"w x 5.63"d. Female, 3.25"h x 2.5"w x 7.75"d. Backstamps: 65.019. Male, $150-200; female, $100-150.

Figurine (F.51). 8.0"h x 7.75"w x 9.13"d.
Backstamp: 65.019. $350-450.

Figurine (F.54). 7.75"h x 3.5"w x
3.25"d. Backstamp: 54.0. $800+

Alternate view (F.54A) of figurine
in F.54.

Figurine (F.52). 3.63"h x 2.63"w x 5.25"d.
Backstamp: 78.9. $100-150.

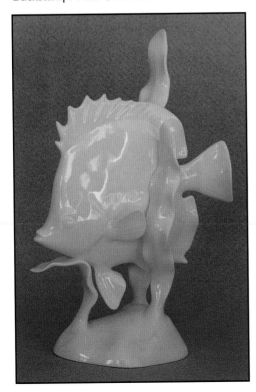

Figurine (F.53). 8.13"h x 5.0"w x 2.5"d.
Backstamp: 65.5. $100-150.

Figurine (F.55). 9.0"h x 3.0"w x 4.75"d.
Backstamp: 65.5. $80-150.

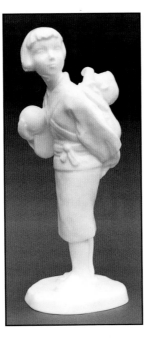

Figurine (F.56). 8.38"h x 3.0"w x 3.38"d. Backstamp: 65.019. $150-250.

Figurine (F.59). 7.5"h x 5.5"w. Backstamp: 67.019. $150-250.

Figurine (F.57). 8.38"h x 6.13"w x 4.5"d. Backstamp: 33.056. $230-330.

Figurine (F.60). Head only, 5.0"h x 4.0"w x 4.0"d. Backstamp: AP75.5 (Arnold Palmer Collection. A Limited Edition of 300 pieces). $50-100.

Figurine (F.58). 8.88"h x 6.25"w x 4.75"d. Backstamp: 33.056. $200-300.

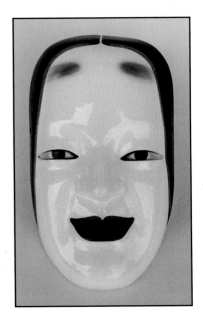

Figurine (F.61). 7.88"h x 4.75"w x 2.25"d. Backstamp: 67.019. $150+

Figurine (F.62). 6.13"h x 8.5"w x 4.0"d. Backstamp: 69.9 (ani-mates). $40-90.

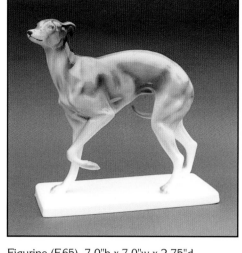

Figurine (F.65). 7.0"h x 7.0"w x 2.75"d. Backstamp: 65.019. $150-250.

Figurine (F.63). 5.38"h x 7.75"w x 3.75"d. Backstamp: 69.9 (ani-mates). $40-90.

Figurines (F.66). Horses, 3.75"h x 5.0"w x 2.75"d. Dogs, 4.75"h x 6.5"w x 3.38"d. Cats, 4.13"h x 4.25"w x 3.63"d. Backstamps: 72.7 (Mother's Day Series: Horse, one of 2800 pieces, 1975, 2nd edition; cat, one of 2800 pieces, 1976, 3rd edition; dog, one of 2800 pieces, 1977, 4th edition). Each, $50-150.

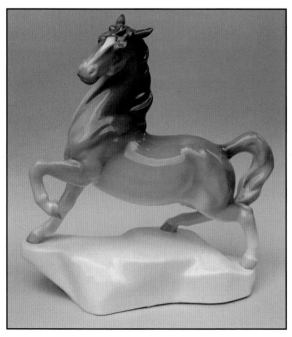

Figurine (F.64). 8.5"h x 8.0"w. Backstamp: 67.019. $100-200.

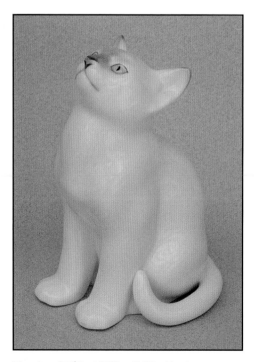

Figurine (F.67). 4.25"h x 3.0"w. Backstamp: 78.9. $100-200.

Chapter L

Lamps, Night lights and Candle holders

Although it is not made explicit in the list below, the items shown in the photos of this chapter are clustered into two groups: items that need candles in order to be lights and those that need bulbs. Within each of those tacit subgroups, the items are sorted into two types that are sequenced alphabetically:

Candlesticks (pp.146-147)
Chambersticks (p.148)
Lamps (pp.148-149)
Night light (p.149)

There are some very nice pairs of candlesticks in this chapter. Finding a matching pair with both in fine condition continues to be a more difficult project than one would think it should be. I have no idea why. The pairs shown in seven of the first eight photos (L.57-L.61 and L.63-L.64) are quite different in style and make an interesting group for that reason. The two candlesticks shown in L.59 *do* match; they have been arranged to show all components of the motif. With a matching round bowl, the three items together would be considered a "console set"—i.e., a grouping intended for display on a dining table before, during and/or after dinner. The candlesticks in L.64 are also arranged so the motif can be seen fully and appreciated all the more. After seeing my photo of them, the owner commented that the one on the right looks like a bizarre face. I would have to agree. The array of tulip candlesticks shown in L.62 is impressive for several reasons, not least being that they are all in one collection. Photo L.7 in my first Noritake book shows a pair that is unlike any of the ones shown in L.62 and I have seen one other motif on this blank. So this makes eight different ones that I know of. One wonders: how many others are there?

The lamps shown are also diverse. One of the more interesting photos is L.74, which shows a nice conceptual set (see the Introduction to Part Two, above). The lamp "vase" shown in L.75 is clearly a factory-made lamp body. Notice that the backstamp (see L.75A) is *beside* the hole that has been drilled to allow a user to install various parts so that it can become a lamp. Notice also the partially closed top to the "vase." This is the only factory-made lamp body I have seen that is like this but it should be emphasized that my lamp sample, even after more than 20 years of active collecting, is modest. Lamps are sometimes seen with a (sometimes nicely) drilled hole right through the backstamp, thus making it rather clear that the drilling was done after the item left the factory. I am asked from time to time whether there is an impact on value when there is evidence that a vase has been drilled after it left Nagoya. My tentative answer is that the impact is negligible *if* the drilling (a) has produced a very round and smooth hole, (b) has not obliterated the backstamp entirely and, most important, (c) has not caused the vase to crack or chip. Even so, it also should be noted that there seems to be more collector interest in "vases" (without holes) than in "lamp vases" (vases with a cord hole).

Finally, I direct your attention to the night light shown in the last photo of the chapter (F.76). It is an amazing piece and one of the rarest items shown in this book. For obvious reasons, Takahiro (Kazuo) Morikawa featured the same lamp on the cover of his recent book *Masterpieces of Early Noritake* (see *Bibliography*).

Candlesticks (L.57). 9.13"h x 4.38"w.
Backstamps: 27.0. Each, $30-40.

Candlesticks (L.58). 8.0"h x 4.88"w.
Backstamps:27.0. Each, $50-80.

Candlesticks (L.59). 6.25"h x 4.38"d. Backstamps: 27.0. Each, $30-40.

Candlesticks (L.62). 5.5"h x 3.38"w. Backstamps: *Second from right*, 19.0; *others* 27.1. Each, $60-90.

Candlesticks (L.60). 6.13"h x 4.38"w. Backstamps: 27.0. Each, $30-40.

Candlesticks (L.63). 3.5"h x 4.25"w. Backstamps: 29.1 (33519). Each, $30-50.

Candlesticks (L.61). 5.25"h x 3.75"w. Backstamps: 27.0. Each, $20-30.

Candlesticks (L.64). 3.5"h x 4.25"w. Backstamps: 27.1. Each, $40-60.

Chambersticks (L.65). 6.25"h x 5.5"w. Backstamps: 27.0. Each, $40-70.

Chambersticks (L.66). 4.0"h x 4.13"w x 4.0"d. Backstamps: 27.0. Each, $50-90.

Chambersticks (L.67). 4.5"h x 4.0"w. Backstamps: 27.0. *Left*, $50-90; *others*, $30-40.

Chambersticks (L.68). 2.25"h x 3.25"w. Backstamps: 27.1. Each, $20-40.

Chamberstick (L.69). 1.63"h x 3.0"w. Backstamp: 27.1. $20-40.

Chamberstick (L.70). 1.5"h x 3.0"w. Backstamp: 27.0. $20-40.

Lamp (L.71). Overall, 20.25"h. Lamp vase, 8.75"h x 5.25"w. Backstamp: 27.0. For lamp vase only, $70-140.

Lamp (L.72). Overall, 14.5"h. Lamp vase, 7.13"h x 3.88"w. Backstamp: 27.0. For lamp vase only, $60-120.

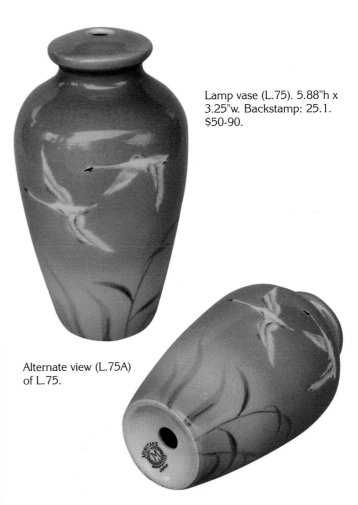

Lamp vase (L.75). 5.88"h x 3.25"w. Backstamp: 25.1. $50-90.

Alternate view (L.75A) of L.75.

Lamp (L.73). Overall, 14.63"h. Lamp vase, 6.0"h x 3.75"w x 3.25"d. Backstamp: Unmarked (The vase has a post-production hole drilled where the backstamp was.) For lamp vase only, $60-120.

Lamps (L.74). Overall, 12.5"h. Candlestick, 6.13"h x 4.25"w. Backstamps: 27.0. Each, $80-130.

Nightlight (L.76). 10.0"h x 8.5"w x 4.0"d. Backstamp: 16.4. $2500+

Plaques, Plates, Trays and Other Flat Items

In this chapter, the many plates, plaques, trays, serving plates and other basically flat items shown in it are grouped as follows:

The list of item types shown in this chapter is more elaborate and detailed than those in my previous Noritake books. I was able (indeed I was forced) to develop this improved list because I now have so many more Chapter P photos on file than in the past. The approximately 125 photos (plus some associated alternative and detail views) shown in this chapter were picked from a file of at least 700 different potential Chapter P photos. With such a large corpus of materials, I felt that the only practical way to select anything like a representative sample would be to first group the photos into more precisely defined types and kinds. The list above is a product of that effort and with it, users of this book will find that it is much easier to find photos of the items they are interested in seeing.

Items of the sort shown in the photos of this chapter appeal to collectors for all sorts of reasons, of course, but three stand out. First, many of these items are relatively large and so the motifs on them often have a lot of **POW**er. Second, a rather high percent of these items were painted completely by hand (free hand), adding to their desirability as a collectible. Third, they are, inch for inch, among the most economical of collectible Noritake fancyware items from the 1921-1931 period. Those who are on a tight budget or at an early stage in their collecting will find that plaques, cake plates and some trays, for example, are among the best bargains in all of "Noritake-land." There are definite exceptions, of course, with the outstanding and extremely rare cake set shown in P.282 being a prime example. But the very next plate (P.283), one that is both beautiful and rather rare, typically sells for less than a tenth of the previous set. The same can be said of the three plates that come after it (P.284-P.286), plus nearly all of the others. How could a collector who likes bold and unusual floral motifs pass up a plate like the one shown in P.288?

The plate shown in P.287 is interesting visually and for other reasons as well. In *Collecting Noritake A to Z*, a similar plate is shown (P.140 on p.125). The central figures are exactly the same as are many of the other main elements of the motif (the lanterns, boats and shoreline), but the upper part of the sky in P.140 is yellow whereas in the one in this chapter it is blue. Given what has been said about conceptual sets (see the Introduction to Part Two), one should predict that a plate like this will turn up with a red sky. What fun it would be to find it and then to see all three of these plates in one place at one time. Until that happens, the reader can get a sense of what such "gatherings" look like by examining some of the other photos of this chapter for, as it happens, quite a few complete conceptual sets are shown. For examples, see P.303, P.306, P.308, P.364, P.368 and P.371-P.372 (taken together). For those who are wondering why P.307 was not included in the previous list it is because, ideally, the third member of that set should be a green *luster* lemon plate. Quite a few incomplete conceptual sets are also shown in this chapter. Readers who are willing to use their imagination should look at the following photos and try to visualize what the missing member of the set will (or should) look like: P.310, P.311, P.351 and P.352 (taken together), P.369 and P.370 (taken together) and P.400.

Two of the lemon plates shown in this book are very unusual. The first of these, shown in P.301, is large enough that some will insist that it isn't even a lemon plate. Since I discussed that issue in *Noritake Fancyware A to Z*, I will not go into it here. And besides, what should really be holding our attention is the outstanding, and also somewhat mysterious, motif that is on this item. We are likely to be far less puzzled by the superb motif on the next lemon plate (P.302). Another item with a superb motif is the cheese server shown in P.316, an item photographed by a collector in Australia. Some items are unusual because of the motif, others because of the blank itself. The item shown in P.319 is an outstanding example of the latter. Noritake fancyware items with attached wicker or metal handles are not all that common but they are not considered rare, either. In my experience, however, it is extremely rare to find an item with porcelain attach points for the handle, as in the example under discussion. As can be seen in P.319A, the handle is divided so that each half can lie flat on the plate, thus making it easy for the user to select a morsel from the area around the edge and dip it into the sauce in the attached dish at the center. Although it is only a surmise on my part, I will venture the opinion that these handles were attached in Japan. I base this on the fact that they are attached to the plate in exactly the same way that wicker handles are attached to Japanese teapots.

Plaques offer all of the advantages plates and trays offer plus one additional one: they are easy to display. This is because, by definition, plaques have factory made holes in the foot rim that allow one easily to use a string or wire to hang them on a wall. There are many incredible plaques shown here, starting with the two newer and exceptionally large ones that open this section of the chapter (P.328 and P.329). I find myself drawn to the plaques in P.334, P.335 and P.347 because of their artistic merit; they are fabulous, don't you think? Two of the other outstanding items shown in this chapter that deserve special comment are the plates shown in P.374 and P.376. These are individual serving plates that go with cake plates, but what do the master plates look like? It may seem that the plate in P.374 would go with the master plate shown in P.137 of *Collecting Noritake A to Z* (p.123) but the rim on that plate is green not yellow and the main color of the lady's gown is peach, not red. Can we take this plate as an indication that there is a version of the cake plate in P.137 with a yellow rim? Similarly, we may ask, in light of the small plate in P.376, what will the master plate look like? Or, alternatively, is it part of a child's tea or cake set? Finally, I direct your attention to the plate shown in P.390. The motif on it is the same as the motif on the ashtray shown above in A.219. The photos of that item should have indicated that it is an exceptionally beautiful piece. The photos of the plate, however, offer not only a better view of the motif but also show quite convincingly why many collectors like "big canvas" Noritake: the larger versions of the motifs found on them usually are stunningly beautiful.

Cake plate (P.278). 1.38"h x 11.13"w. Backstamp: 27.1. $40-70.

Cake plate (P.279). 1.5"h x 10.88"w x 9.5"d. Backstamp: 27.0. $30-60.

Cake plate (P.280). 1.0"h x 10.5"w x 9.25"d.
Backstamp: 25.1. $30-60.

Cake set (P.282). Cake plate, 1.0"h x 10.63"w. Individual
plates, .75"h x 6.5"dia. Backstamps: 27.0. Complete set
as shown, $700+

Detail (P.280A) of P.280.

Cake plate (P.283). 1.0"h x 10.13"w x 9.5"d. Backstamp:
27.0. $30-50.

Cake plate (P.281). 1.25"h x 10.25"w x 9.88"d.
Backstamp: 27.1. $50-80.

Cake plate (P.284). 1.0"h x 10.25"w x 9.5"d. Backstamp:
27.1. $30-50.

Cake plate (P.285). 1.0"h x 10.0"w x 9.75"d.
Backstamp: 19.1. $30-60.

Cake plate (P.287). 1.13"h x 10.25"w x 9.5"d.
Backstamp: 27.0. $60-80.

Detail (P.285A) of P.285.

Detail (P.287A) of P.287.

Cake plate (P.286). 9.75"w x 9.5"d.
Backstamp: 27.0. $40-70.

Cake plate (P.288). 1.25"h x 9.75"w x 9.25"d.
Backstamp: 07.0. $40-60.

Cake plate (P.289). 1.15"h x 9.75"w x 9.5"d.
Backstamp: 27.1. $40-60.

Cake plate
(P.292). 1.0"h x
10.75"w x
10.25"d.
Backstamp:
27.1. $20-40.

Cake plate (P.290). 9.75"w x 9.5"d.
Backstamp: 27.1. $20-40.

Cake plate (P.293).
1.13"h x 9.38"w x
9.13"d.
Backstamp: 19.2.
$40-60.

Cake plate
(P.294). 1.5"h x
10.75"w x
10.0"d.
Backstamp:
27.1. $30-50.

Cake plate (P.291). 1.25"h x 9.63"w x 9.38"d.
Backstamp: 16.0. $20-40.

Detail (P.294A) of P.294.

154

Cake plates (P.295). 1.25"h x 9.75"w x 9.5"d. Backstamps: 27.1. $20-30.

Cake plate (P.296). 1.13"h x 9.63"w x 8.5"d. Backstamp: 14.0. $170-270.

Detail (P.296A) of P.296.

Cake plate (P.297). 1.13"h x 9.0"w x 8.88"d. Backstamp: ML21.1. $20-40.

Loop center-handled lemon plates (P.298). 2.75"h x 5.25"dia. Backstamps: 27.1. Each, $20-30.

Loop center-handled lemon plates (P.299). 2.38"h x 5.25"dia. Backstamps: 27.1. Each, $20-30.

Loop center-handled lemon plates (P.300). 1.38"h x 5.13"w x 5.13"d. Backstamps: *Left,* 58.0; *right,* 25.1. Each, $20-30.

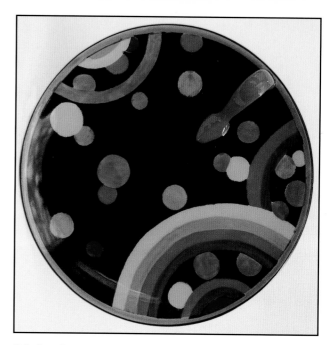

Side-handled lemon plate (P.302). 1.25"h x 6.25"dia. Backstamp: 27.1. $50-90.

Side-handled lemon plate (P.301). 1.75"h x 7.63"dia. Backstamp: 27.1. $400+

Side-handled lemon plates (P.303). 1.13"h x 5. 63"dia. Backstamps: 27.1. Each, $20-30.

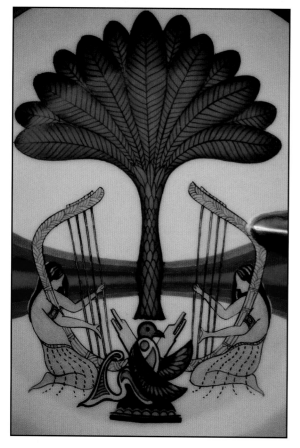

Detail (P.301A) of P.301.

Side-handled lemon plates (P.304). 1.13"h x 5.63"dia. Backstamps: 27.1. Each, $20-30.

Side-handled sided lemon plates (P.305). 1.25"h x 5.5"dia. Backstamps: 27.1. Each, $20-40.

Side-handled lemon plates (P.308). 1.38"h x 5.5"w. Backstamps: 27.1. Each, $20-30.

Side-handled lemon plates (P.306). 1. 38"h x 5.88"d. Backstamps: 27.1. Each, $20-30.

Side-handled lemon plates (P.309). 1. 63"h x 6.5"w x 5.25"d. Backstamp: *Upper left,* 32.456; *upper right* 58.0; *others,* 54.0. Each, $20-40.

Side-handled lemon plates (P.307). 1.38"h x 5.88"d. Backstamps: 27.1. Each, $20-30.

Side-handled lemon plates (P.310). 1.25"h x 5.75"w. Backstamps: 27.1. Each, $20-30.

Side-handled lemon plates (P.311). 1.13"h x 5.38"w x 4.0"d. Backstamps: 27.1. Each, $20-40.

Solid center-handled, sided lemon plates (P.314). 3.0"h x 5.75"w. Backstamps: 27.0. Each, $20-30.

Solid center-handled lemon plate (P.312). 2.25"h x 5.75"w. Backstamp: 27.0. $20-30.

Solid center-handled lemon plates (P.315). 1.75"h x 6.25"dia. Backstamps: 27.1. *Left*, each, $30-50; *right*, each, $20-30.

Solid center-handled lemon plates (P.313). 2.25"h x 6.0"w. Backstamp: 27.1. Each, $20-30.

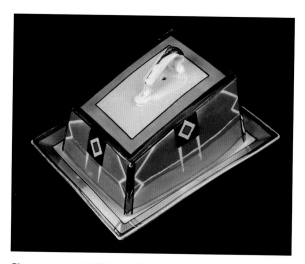

Cheese server (P.316). 3.5"h x 6.0"w x 5.0"d. Backstamp: 79.0. $80-140.

Chip and dip set (P.317). 4.5" h x 9.5"w. Backstamp: 27.0. $400-800.

Chip and dip plate (P.319) with attached metal handles. 2.6"h x 9.0"w. Backstamp: 27.1. $120-190.

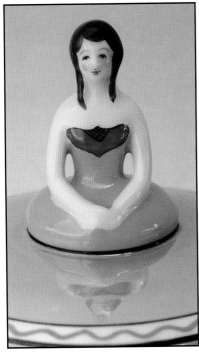

Detail (P.317A) of P.317.

Alternate handles-down view (P.319A) of P.319.

Chip and dip (P.318) (one piece). 2.6"h x 9.0"w. Backstamp: 27.0. $40-80.

Multi-piece serving set (P.320). Serving bowl, 1.63"h x 12.0"w x 9.5"d. Sauce pitcher, 3.63"h x 6.5"w x 3.13"d. Plate, .88"h x 7.38"w. Servers, 7.25"long. Backstamps: 27.1 Complete set, as shown, $190-240.

Serving set with matching ladle (P.321). 4.25"h x 10.75"w. Backstamps: Plate unmarked; bowl and ladle, 27.1 Complete set, as shown, $150-210.

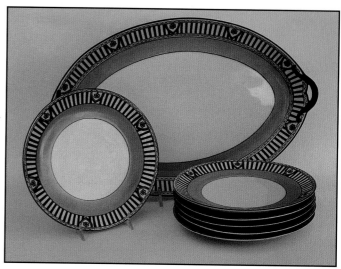

Serving set (P.324) with platter. Platter, 1.5"h x 13.88"w x 8.75"d. Individual plates, .75"h x 6.25"dia. Backstamps: 27.0. Complete set, as shown, $100-150.

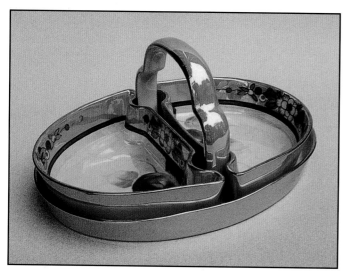

Serving set (P.322). 3.5"h x 8.25"w x 6.13"d. Backstamps: 19.1 $40-80.

Serving set (P.325) with tray. Tray, .75"h x 11.25"w x 5.75"d. Plates, .75"h x 5.75"w x 5.75"d. Backstamps: Tray, 15.01; plates, 16.0. Complete set, as shown, $140-190.

Serving set (P.323). Overall, 1.25"h x 8.25"dia. Insert, 1.13"h x 5.75"w x 2.75"d. Backstamps: 27.0. $40-80.

Pancake server (P.326). 3.25"h x 7.88"dia. Backstamp: 26.0. $40-80.

Sweetmeat set (P.327). Center dish, 4.5"w x 4.5"d. Box, 1.63"h x 9.25"dia. Backstamps: 27.0 $80-150.

Plaque (P.330), molded in relief. 1.38"h x 10.63"dia. Backstamp: 27.0. $200-400.

Plaque (P.328). 1.5"h x 13.88"dia. Backstamp: 74.7. $120-220.

Plaque (P.331). 10.25"dia. Backstamp: 27.0. $140-200.

Plaque (P.329). 1.38"h x 14.13"dia. Backstamp: 50.3. $120-220.

Plaque (P.332). 1.13"h x 9.88"dia. Backstamp: 07.0. $90-150.

Plaque (P.333). 1.0"h x 10.75"dia. Backstamp: 77.3. $90-150.

Plaque (P.334). 1.38"h x 10.25"dia. Backstamp: 27.0. $80-140.

Detail (P.334A) of P.334.

Plaque (P.335). 1.25"h x 10.13"dia. Backstamp: 27.0. $100-190.

Detail (P.335A) of P.335.

Plaque (P.336). 1.5"h x 14.13"dia. Backstamp: 07.7. $120-220.

Detail (P.336A) of P.336.

Plaque (P.337). Signed by Keshi. .88"h x 10.75"dia. Backstamp: 74.5. $20-50.

Plaque (P.340). Signed by Y. Kobayashi. 1.0"h x 10.63"dia. Backstamp: 76.3. $20-50.

Plaque (P.338). 1.0"h x 10.63"dia. Backstamp: 76.3. $20-50.

Plaque (P.341). Signed by K. Rayakawa. 1.0"h x 10.5"dia. Backstamp: 74.5. $20-50.

Plaque (P.339). .88"h x 10.75"dia. Backstamp: 76.3. $20-50.

Plaque (P.342). Signed by J. Takeshi. 1.0"h x 10.5"dia. Backstamp: 74.5. $20-50.

Plaque (P.343). 1.0"h x 7.5"dia. Backstamp: 43.056. $40-60.

Plaque (P.346). Artist, Shazat. .88"h x 10.75"dia. Backstamp: 76.3. $40-70.

Plaque (P.344). .38"h x 6.13"dia. Backstamp: 36.0. $70-120.

Plaque (P.347). 1.13"h x 9.88"dia. Backstamp: 50.3. $90-170.

Plaque (P.345). Artist, Terano. .88"h x 10.75"dia. Backstamp: 76.3. $40-70.

Detail (P.347A) of P.347.

Plate (P.348), center-handled, with figural element. 5.5"h x 9.5"dia. Backstamp: 19.1. $160-210.

Plate (P.349) with metal handle. 5.13"h x 10.0"dia. Backstamp: 27.1. $30-40.

Plate (P.350) with bolted metal stand. 5.25"h x 8.63"dia. Backstamp: 16.4. $80-120.

Alternate view (P.350A) of P.350.

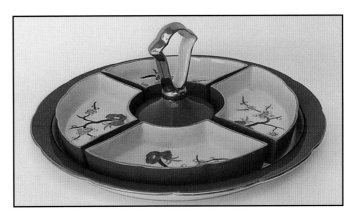

Plate (P.351), center-handled, with four inserts. 4.0"h x 10.0"w. Backstamp: 27.1. $60-100.

Plate (P.352), center-handled, with four inserts. 4.0"h x 10.0"w. Backstamp: 27.1. $60-100.

Plate (P.353), center-handled. 4.0"h x 9.75"dia. Backstamp: 27.0. $40-90.

165

Plate (P.354), center-handled. 3.75"h x 9.62"dia.
Backstamp: 27.0. $40-90.

Plates (P.357), center-handled. 2.75"h x 7.5"dia. Backstamps: 27.1.
Each, $30-40.

Sandwich plates (P.358). 2.75"h x 7.5"dia. Backstamps: 27.1.
Each, $20-40.

Sandwich plate (P.355). 3.25"h x 8.0"dia. Backstamp: 27.1.
$50-100.

Sided plate (P.359), center-handled. 3.38"h x 9.25"w.
Backstamp: 25.1. $110-160.

Plate (P.356), center-handled. 2.75"h x 7.5"dia.
Backstamp: 29.1. $30-60.

Sided plate (P.360), center-handled. 4.0"h x 9.13"w x 9.13"d.
Backstamp: 25.1. $50-80.

Sided plate (P.361), center-handled. 3.5"h x 9.0"w.
Backstamp: 27.1. $40-70.

Plates (P.364). .88"h x 7.63"dia. Backstamps: 27.0.
Each, $30-50.

Plates (P.362). .75"h x 6.25"dia. Backstamps: 27.0.
Each, $100-200.

Plate (P.365). .75"h x 7.5"dia. Backstamp: 27.0.
$20-30.

Plates (P.363). 1.0"h x 8.63"dia. Backstamps: 27.0.
Each, $20-40.

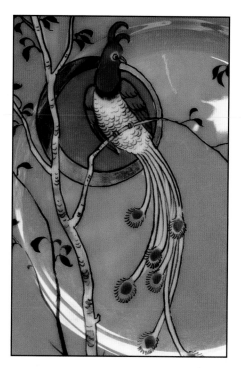

Detail (P.365A)
of P.365.

Plate (P.366). .63"h x 6.25"dia. Backstamp: 27.1. $90-180.

Detail (P.368A) of P.368 (*upper left*).

Plate (P.367). .63"h x 6.25"dia. Backstamp: 27.1. $90-180.

Detail (P.368B) of P.368 (*upper right*).

Plates (P.368). .75"h x 6.38"dia. Backstamps: 27.0. Each, $40-70.

Detail (P.368C) of P.368 (*bottom*).

Plate (P.369). 1.0"h x 11.25"dia. Backstamp: 43.056.
$50-80.

Plate (P.371). 1.0"h x 8.63"dia. Backstamp: 27.1. $400-600.

Detail (P.369A) of P.369.

Plate (P.372). 1.0"h x 8.5"dia. Backstamp: 27.1. $350-500.

Plate (P.370). 1.0"h x 11.25"dia. Backstamp: 43.056.
$50-80.

Plate (P.373). 1.0"h x 8.63"dia. Backstamp: 27.1. $350-500.

Plate (P.374). .88"h x 7.25"dia. Backstamp: 27.1. $50+

Plate (P.375). The scoreboard shows that it is 3 to 1 in the top of the 4th inning. .88"h x 6.63"dia. Backstamp: 49.456. $20-30.

Plate (P.376). .75"h x 6.5"dia. Backstamp: 27.0. $50+

Detail (P.374A) of P.374.

Detail (P.376A) of P.376.

170

Plates (P.377). 1.0"h x 7.63"dia. Backstamps: 27.0. Each, $20-50.

Plates (P.378). 1.0"h x 7.63"dia. Backstamps: 27.1. Each, $20-50.

Plates (P.379). .75"h x 6.38"dia. Backstamps: 27.0. Each, $20-50.

Plates (P.380). .88"h x 7.63"dia. Backstamps: 27.0. Each, $20-30.

Plates (P.381). .88"h x 7.63"dia. Backstamps: 27.0. Each, $20-30.

Sided plate (P.382). 1.0"h x 8.5"w x 8.5"d. Backstamp: 25.1. $30-40.

Sided plate (P.383). 1.0"h x 5.75"w. Backstamp: 58.1. $20-30.

Plate (P.386) with two handles. 1.13"h x 7.88"w x 7.38"d. Backstamp: 27.1. $20-40.

Plates (P.384) with one side handle. 1.13" h x 7.5"w x 7.25"d. Backstamps: 27.0. Each, $20-40.

Plates (P.387) with two handles. 1.13"h x 7.75"w x 7.25"d. Backstamps: 27.1. Each, $20-40.

Plate (P.385) with two handles. .75"h x 7.75"w x 7.25"d. Backstamp: 27.1. $50-90.

Plates (P.388) with two handles. 1.13"h x 7.63"w x 7.25"d. Backstamps: *Left,* 27.0; *Right,* 27.1. Each, $20-40.

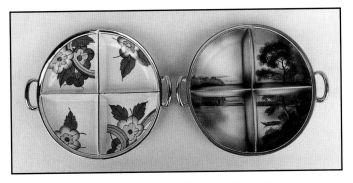

Plates (P.389) with two handles. 1.75"h x 10.5"w 9.0"d. Backstamps: 27.1. Each, $40-90.

Tray (P.391). 1.13"h x 17.25"w x 6.63"d. Backstamp: 27.1. $90-140.

Plate (P.390) with three handles. 2.0"h x 9.25"w. Backstamp: 27.1. $60-110.

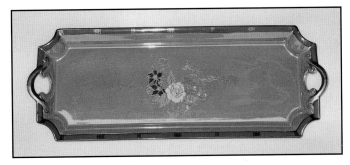

Tray (P.392). 1.13"h x 17.25"w x 6.63"d. Backstamp: 27.1. $40-70.

Tray (P.393). 1.0"h x 12.88"w x 7.38"d. Backstamp: 27.0. $200-350.

Detail (P.390A) of P.390.

Detail (P.393A) of P.393.

Tray (P.394). 1.38"h x 11.13"w x 8.5"d.
Backstamp: 27.0. $50-90.

Tray (P.396). 1.0"h x 10.0"w x 5.0"d. Backstamp: 27.1. $250-400.

Tray (P.395). .63"h x 12.0"w. Backstamp: 19.0.
$60-120.

Tray (P.397). .88"h x 8.88"w x 8.88"d.
Backstamp: 27.1. $180-280.

Detail (P.395A)
of P.395.

Detail (P.397A)
of P.397.

174

Tray (P.398). .88"h x 9.0"w x 9.0"d. Backstamp: 27.0. $110-190.

Detail (P.398A) of P.398.

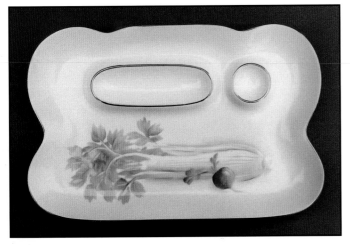

Snack tray (P.399). 1.0"h x 9.75"w x 6.25"d. Backstamp: 16.0. $30-50.

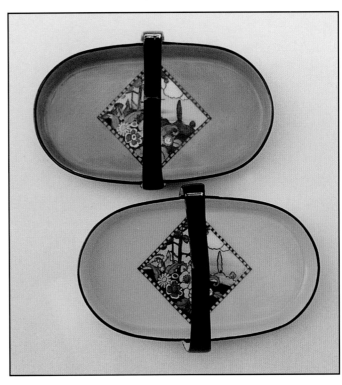

Trays (P.400). 3.13"h x 6.63"w x 4.13"d. Backstamps: 27.1. Each, $40-80.

Tray (P.401). 1.25"h x 7.75"w x 3.5"d. Backstamp: 27.1. $200-300.

Tray (P.402). .38"h x 6.75"w x 4.13"d. Backstamp: 27.0. $20-30.

Salesman Sample Pages

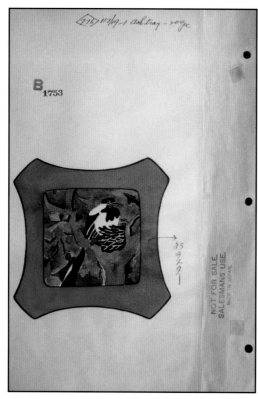

Noritake
salesman
sample book
page (S.22).
11.5"h x 7.5"w.

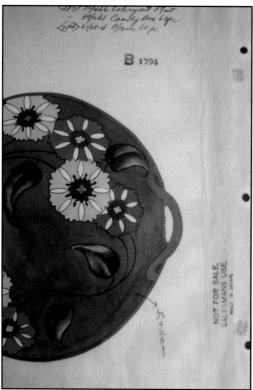

Noritake
salesman
sample book
page (S.23).
11.5"h x 7.5"w.

The items shown in this chapter are pages from Noritake "salesman sample books." In North America, these pages apparently are extremely rare or, to be more precise, *very* few of the Noritake collectors that I know have any. (I have no idea how many are owned by collectors of paper.) I am particularly grateful, therefore, to Dr. and Mrs. Dennis Buonafede for permitting me to take photographs of some of the salesman sample pages in their collection and for agreeing to let them be shown in this book.

These items date to the period before World War II when sales personnel working on behalf of the Noritake Company would travel around North America carrying loose-leaf notebooks filled with a hundred or so pages like those shown in these photos. Such notebooks were used to show prospective retailers what could be ordered. Because it was a loose-leaf notebook, a salesman could easily add and delete pages as the possibilities changed. (A photo of such a book is shown in *Noritake Collectibles A to Z*, photo 2.19, page 19.) Typically, these pages were 11.5" high and 7.5" wide overall. They were not printed but, rather, each page was painted individually and by hand. To the collector today, this is important and impressive.

Collectors like seeing these materials for several other reasons. A primary one is that it is both fun and interesting if one can match a page to an actual Noritake piece. Most of us, unfortunately, can expect to do this only by comparing pieces (or photos of them) to photos of salesman sample pages, not the actual pages. In this book, the ashtray shown in A.228 is also shown in the first salesman sample page shown in this chapter (S.22). An alternative to this endeavor is to ignore the particulars of the blank shown on a salesman sample page and, instead, search for (a photo of) a Noritake fancyware item that has the same *motif*. There is an example of this in the photos of these pages: the motif on the bowl in S.23 can be seen also on the relish set shown in B.703. On rare occasions, we can actually put the piece and the matching page together at the same time. Two examples of this are shown in *Collecting Noritake A to Z* (p.147). In instances where this has happened, we see that the painted pages show the objects at full size. Most if not all the other salesman sample pages apparently were made this way as well. This is why many of the pages do not show the entire item. Also, the colors on the pages are very close to those that appear on the actual pieces. Although this is what one would expect, it is not something that could simply be presumed prior to having the piece right next to the painted page. Speaking for myself, however, one of the best things about such pages is that a fair number of the ones we have seen show items and/or motifs that we do not yet know of on Noritake fancyware available in the secondary market. To the optimists, this will mean that items with those shapes and motifs *should* be out there waiting for us to discover them. Happy hunting!

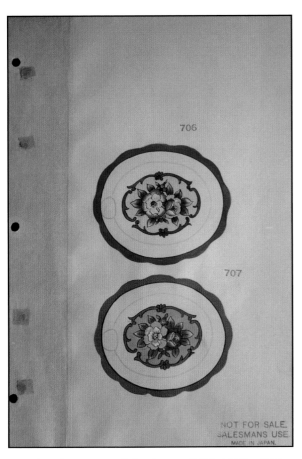

Noritake salesman sample book page (S.24). 11.5"h x 7.5"w.

Noritake salesman sample book page (S.26). 11.5"h x 7.5"w.

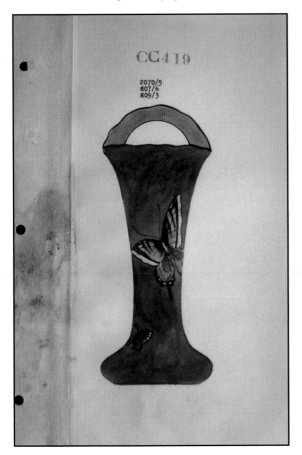

Noritake salesman sample book page (S.25). 11.5"h x 7.5"w.

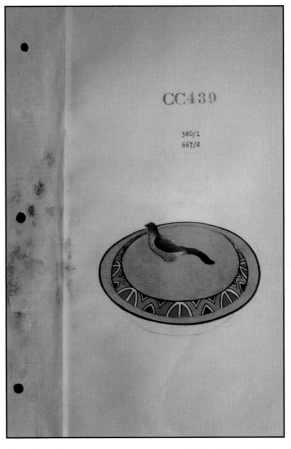

Noritake salesman sample book page (S.27). 11.5"h x 7.5"w.

Noritake salesman sample book page (S.28). 11.5"h x 7.5"w.

Noritake salesman sample book page (S.30). 11.5"h x 7.5"w.

Noritake salesman sample book page (S.29). 11.5"h x 7.5"w.

Noritake salesman sample book page (S.31). 11.5"h x 7.5"w.

178

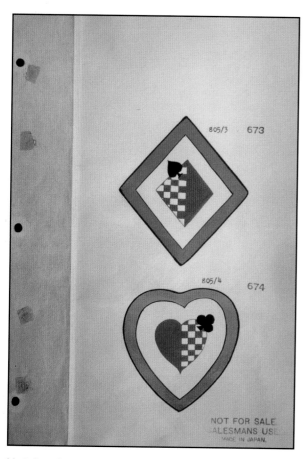

Noritake salesman sample book page (S.32). 11.5"h x 7.5"w.

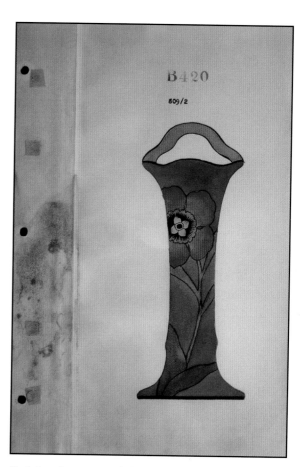

Noritake salesman sample book page (S.34). 11.5"h x 7.5"w.

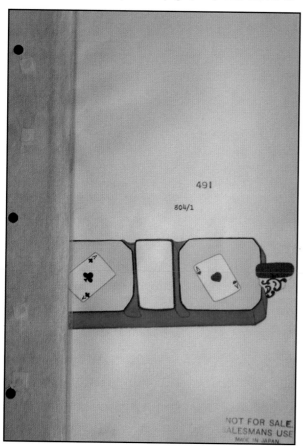

Noritake salesman sample book page (S.33). 11.5"h x 7.5"w.

Noritake salesman sample book page (S.35). 11.5"h x 7.5"w.

Noritake salesman sample book page (S.36). 11.5"h x 7.5"w.

Noritake salesman sample book page (S.38). 11.5"h x 7.5"w.

Noritake salesman sample book page (S.37). 11.5"h x 7.5"w.

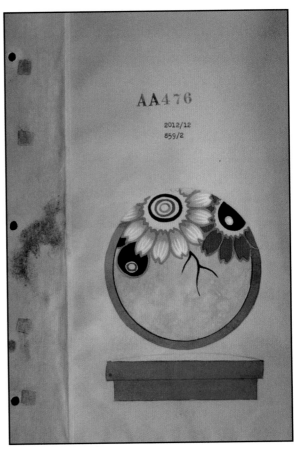

Noritake salesman sample book page (S.39). 11.5"h x 7.5"w.

Noritake salesman sample book page (S.40). 11.5"h x 7.5"w.

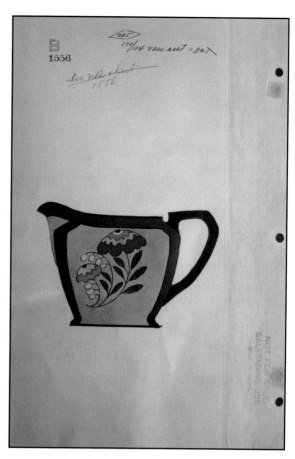

Noritake salesman sample book page (S.42). 11.5"h x 7.5"w.

Noritake salesman sample book page (S.41). 11.5"h x 7.5"w.

Noritake salesman sample book page (S.43). 11.5"h x 7.5"w.

Tea Sets and Other Items Pertaining to Beverages

Tea sets and related items that pertain to beverages in one way or another are the focus of this chapter. The photographs of the items shown are grouped and sequenced as follows:

Breakfast set (p.182)
Child's tea set (p.183)
Chocolate set (p.183)
Coffee pot and demitasse sets (pp.183-184)
Coridal set (p.184)
Cream and sugar sets (pp.184-187)
Ewer (p.188)
Snack sets (p.188)
Tea pot and sets (pp.188-189)
Tea strainers (p.189)
Tea tiles and trivets (pp.189-190)

Some interesting and elegant items are shown in this chapter. One of the rarest, surely, is the child's tea set shown in T.158. Even the box is in almost perfect condition and the porcelain items look as though they had never been removed from it. It is nice to be able to show demitasse and coffee sets that are complete (e.g., T.163) but two truly amazing incomplete coffee sets (T.161 and T.162) demonstrate quite convincingly that photos of less than complete sets can be *very* satisfying. But many will feel (as I do) that even those wonderful sets pale in the face of the dramatic demitasse set shown in T.166. Cordial sets, such as the one shown in T.167, are very rare and, so far, I have never seen one that has a full set of cups (six at least).

Cream and sugar sets, on the other hand, are as common as rain in a Seattle winter. That does not mean, however, that they are not desirable for collectors. The many rare and beautiful sets shown in this chapter should make that abundantly clear. The most unusual one, I think, is shown in T.168. Some may wonder whether this is a true set. To see why I think it is, one need only look at T.168B. Notice, first, that there is an unusual rim on the bottom of both the creamer and underplate—rims that are seldom (if ever) seen on other similar-sized Noritake creamers and plates. The rim of the creamer fits perfectly inside the top of the sugar bowl and the plate rim fits snugly on top of the creamer (as shown). Sec-

ond and more significantly, neither the underplate/lid nor the creamer have a backstamp, but the sugar does. Because some pieces in a multi-piece set usually are not marked, I think the backstamp pattern seen here indicates that we are looking at a very unusual Noritake multi-piece cream and sugar set.

When scanning the photos of the cream and sugar sets, many will pause at the figural set shown in T.171 (and for good reason); some may want to pause even longer for the set in T.172 for, in my experience, it is even rarer. One of the most elegant Noritake cream and sugar sets that I know of is shown in T.175 and, right near it, in T.176, is a set with a particularly fine Deco floral motif. The tea set shown in T.195, while not at all Deco, is quite elegant, due to its dramatic shape and the way it has been decorated with etched gold. The set in T.198 is quite rare for the post 1921 era and also quite eye-catching. For those who wonder whether the tea strainer shown in T.200 is a true set, it is important to note that there are no legs on the strainer. This is an important fact because there are legs on the more commonly seen Noritake tea strainers that sit on an under plate. Finally, may I suggest that you pause, when you get there, at T.205, for it provides a great opportunity to reflect on the breadth of the stylistic range offered by Noritake Company items in the 1920s. It is one of the great appeals of Noritake fancyware as a collectible.

Breakfast set (T.157). Tray, 1.5"h x 10.25"w. Tea pot, 3.75"h x 5.5"w x 5.5"w. Toast rack, 1.88"h x 3.0"w x 2.5"d. Cup, 2.5"h x 4.0"w x 3.38"d. Creamer, 2.38"h x 3.5"w. Jelly cup, 1.13"h x 2.0"w. Backstamps: 25.1. Complete, as shown, $90-140.

Child's tea set (T.158) in original box. Cup, 1.25"h x 2.88"w x 2.25"d. Saucer, .63"h x 3.75"dia. Sugar, 2.75"h x 3.63"w x 2.0"d. Creamer, 2.0"h x 2.75"w x 1.75"d. Pot, 3.5"h x 5.25"w x 2.5"d. Plate, .63"h x 4.38"dia. Box, 3.25"h x 12.75"w 11.75"d. Backstamps: 26.0. Set as shown, $400+

Chocolate set (T.159). Pot, 9.0"h x 6.88"w x 3.63"d. Cup, 2.75"h x 3.0"w x 2.25"d. Saucer, .75"h x 4.5"w. Backstamps: 27.0. With service for 6, $250-400.

Coffee pot (T.160). 9.88"h x 9.63"w x 5.38"d. Backstamps: 19.0. $80-120.

Coffee set (T.161). Pot, 6.88"h x 7.13"w x 3.88"d. Creamer, 3.5"h x 4.0"w x 2.75"d. Sugar, 4.13"d x 5.13"w x 3.25"d. Backstamps: 27.0. Items shown, $200-250.

Demitasse set (T.162). Coffee set. Pot, 6.88"h x 7.13"w x 3.88"d. Creamer, 3.5"h x 4.0"w x 2.75"d. Sugar, 4.13"d x 5.13"w x 3.25"d. Backstamps: 27.0. Items shown, $450+

Demitasse set (T.163). Tray, .5"h x 12.0" dia. Creamer, 3.0"h x 3.5"w x 2.5"d. Sugar, 3.88"h x 4.75"w x 3.0"d. Cup, 2.75"h x 2.88"w x 2.13"d. Saucer, 1.5"h x 4.5"dia. Pot, 7.13"h x 6.63"w x 3.25"d. Backstamps: 25.1. With service for 6, $200-250.

Demitasse set (T.164). Pot, 6.5"h x 7.13"w x 3.5"d. Sugar, 4.0"h x 5.25"w. Creamer, 3.5"h x 4.13"w. Tray, .5"h x 12.0"dia. Backstamps: 27.0. With service for 6, $450-600.

Demitasse set (T.165). Sugar, 4.0"h x 5.25"w x 3.5"d. Pot, 7.13"h x 7.13"w x 4.0"d. Creamer, 3.0"h x 4.0"w x 3.0"d. Cup and saucer, 2.5"h x 4.5"w. Backstamps: C20.1. With service for 6, $100-200.

Demitasse set (T.166). Pot, 7.0"h x 7.0"w x 3.25"d. Sugar, 3.88"h x 4.5"w. Creamer, 2.75"h x 3.75"w x 2.25"d. Cup, 2.0"h x 3.0"w x 2.38"d. Saucer, .63"h x 4.5"d. Backstamps (*all* items marked): 16.0. With service for 6, $500+

Cordial set (T.167). Bottle, 10.25"h x 4.75"w. Tray, .5"h x 9.75"dia. Cup, 3.63"h x 2.0"w. Backstamps: 27.1. Complete, with service for 6, $500+

Stacking cream and sugar set (T.168). Overall, 4.0"h x 2.88"w. Backstamp (sugar only): 27.1. $50-80.

Alternate view (T.168B) of T.168.

Alternate view (T.168A) of T.168.

Cream and sugar set (T.169). Tray, 1.0"h x 10.75"w. Sugar, 6.13"h x 5.0"w. Creamer, 5.0"h x 3.75"w. Backstamps: 27.0. $80-120.

Cream and sugar set (T.172). Sugar, 4.88"h x 6.25"w x 4.0"d. Creamer, 3.5"h x 5.13"w x 3.38"d. Backstamps: 27.0. $80-160.

Cream and sugar set (T.173). Sugar, 4.0"h x 5.0"w. Creamer, 3.25"h x 4.0"w. Backstamps: 27.1. $50-70.

Cream and sugar set (T.170). Tray, 1.5"h x 11.25"w x 4.0"d. Sugar, 2.38"h x 6.13"w x 3.38"d. Creamer, 3.75"h x 3.88"w x 2.25"d. Backstamps (on all items): 27.1. $80-120.

Cream and sugar set (T.174). Sugar, 4.88"h x 6.88"w x 4.13"d. Creamer, 3.75"h x 5.5"w x 3.38"d. Backstamps: 27.1. $60-90.

Cream and sugar set (T.171). Sugar, 4.88"h x 5.63"w x 3.75"d. Creamer, 3.63"h x 5.13"w x 3.13"d. Backstamps: 27.1. $150-250.

Detail (T.174A) of T.174.

185

Cream and sugar set (T.175), molded-in-relief. Sugar, 4.5"h x 7.0"w x 4.0"d. Creamer, 3.75"h x 6.0"w x 3.5"d. Backstamps: 25.1. $110-190.

Cream and sugar set (T.179). Sugar, 4.5"h x 6.0"w x 3.25"d. Creamer, 3.25"h x 4.5"w x 2.5"d. Backstamps: 27.0. $30-40.

Cream and sugar set (T.176). Sugar, 3.13"h x 6.0"w x 2.88"d. Creamer, 3.75"h x 4.5"w x 2.25"d. Backstamps: 27.1. $60-120.

Cream and sugar set (T.180). Sugar, 4.0"h x 6.25"w x 5.13"d. Creamer, 4.13"h x 5.25"w x 3.5"d. Backstamps: 27.1. $40-60.

Cream and sugar set (T.177). Sugar, 2.5"h x 6.0"w x 3.5"d. Creamer, 3.75"h x 3.88"w x 2.25"d. Backstamps: 27.1. $20-40.

Cream and sugar set (T.181). Sugar, 3.88"h x 6.25"w x 5.25"d. Creamer, 3.5"h x 5.63"w x 4.13"d. Backstamps: 07.0. $40-60.

Cream and sugar set (T.178). Sugar, 3.13"h x 6.0"w. Creamer, 4.25"h x 4.5"w. Backstamps: 25.1. $20-40.

Cream and sugar set (T.182). Sugar, 4.25"h x 6.0"w x 4.38"d. Creamer, 3.88"h x 5.38"w x 3.5"d. Backstamps: 27.1. $30-50.

Cream and sugar set (T.183). Sugar, 3.75"h x 5.88"w x 4.25"d. Creamer, 3.75"h x 5.25"w x 3.75"d. Backstamps: 19.1. $20-40.

Cream and sugar set (T.187). Creamer, 2.75"h x 4.75"w x 3.63"d. Sugar, 3.75"h x 6.0"w x 4.38"d. Backstamps: 27.0. $40-80.

Cream and sugar set (T.184). Sugar, 2.88"h x 5.75"w x 3.5"d. Creamer, 3.88"h x 4.38"w x 2.5"d. Backstamps: 27.1. $30-50.

Cream and sugar set (T.188). Sugar, 4.5"h x 5.75"w. Creamer, 3.5"h x 4.5"w x 3.13"d. Backstamps: 27.0. $30-50.

Cream and sugar set (T.185). Sugar, 2.75"h x 6.0"w x 3.5"d. Creamer, 4.0"h x 4.5"w x 2.63"d. Backstamps: 27.1. $20-40.

Cream and sugar set (T.189). Sugar, 3.25"h x 5.25"w x 3.5"d. Creamer, 2.63 "h x 4.25"w x 3.0"d. Backstamps: 27.0. $30-40.

Cream and sugar set (T.186). Sugar, 2.88"h x 6.0"w x 3.5"d. Creamer, 3.88"h x 4.5"w x 2.63"d. Backstamps: 27.1. $20-40.

Cream and sugar set (T.190). Sugar, 3.38"h x 5.0"w. Creamer, 2.63"h x 3.75"w. Backstamps: 27.0. $20-30.

Ewer (T.191). 10.0"h x 5.5"w x 5.25"d.
Backstamp: 27.1. $100-200.

Tea pot (T.194). 5.0"h x 8.88"w x 5.25"d. Backstamp: 27.0. $40-50.

Snack set (T.192). Tray, .5"h x 8.5"w x 6.25"d. Cup, 2.0"h x 4.13"w x 3.38"d. Backstamp: Tray, unmarked; cup, 27.1. $40-60.

Tea set (T.195). Pot, 5.5"h x 8.5"w x 5.75"d. Creamer, 4.0"h x 4.5"w x 3.75"d. Sugar, 4.75 "h x 6.25"w x 4.5"d. Cup 2.0"h x 4.25"w x 3.75"d. Saucer, .75"h x 5.5"dia. Plate, 1.0"h x 7.5"dia. Backstamps: Saucer, unmarked; all others, 27.0. Service for 6, $230-330.

Snack set (T.193). Plate, .88"h x 8.5"w x 7.38"d. Cup, 1.75"h x 4.0"w x 3.25"d. Backstamp: Plate, unmarked; cup, 27.1. $20-30.

Tea set (T.196). Pot, 5.75"h x 8.5"w x 5.0"d. Creamer, 3.5"h x 4.5"w x 3.38"d. Sugar, 4.5 "h x 6.0"w x 4.0"d. Backstamps: C21.0. Items shown, $90-160.

Tea set (T.197). Pot, 5.75"h x 8.63"w x 4.63"d. Creamer, 3.38"h x 4.88"w x 3.13"d. Sugar, 4.63 "h x 6.13"w x 4.0"d. Cup 2.0"h x 4.5"w x 3.75"d. Saucer, .75"h x 5.5"dia. Plate, .75"h x 7.63"dia. Backstamps: 27.1. Service for 6, $350-450.

Tea strainer (T.200). Footless strainer, .88"h x 5.25"w x 3.63"d. Bowl, 1.75"h x 3.0"w. Backstamp: Strainer, unmarked; bowl, 27.0. $40-80.

Tea set (T.198). Pot, 4.13"h x 8.75"w x 4.75"d. Creamer, 3.0"h x 5.0"w x 3.63"d. Sugar, 4.0 "h x 6.63"w x 4.5"d. Cup 2.0"h x 4.63"w x 3.88"d. Saucer, .75"h x 5.25"dia. Backstamps: 27.0. Service for 6, $500+

Alternate view (T.200A) of T.200.

Tea tile (T.201). 1.0"h x 6.5"dia. Backstamp: 27.0. $50-90.

Tea strainer (T.199). 1.0"h x 5.5"w x 3.75"d. Plate, 4.88"dia. Backstamps: 27.1. $40-70.

Detail (T.201A) of T.201.

Tea tile (T.202). .5"h x 6.5"dia. Backstamp: 27.0. $300-400.

Tea tile (T.204). .63"h x 6.0"dia. Backstamps: 27.0. $90-170.

Tea tile (T.203). .5"h x 6.5"dia. Backstamp: 27.1. $300-400.

Tea tiles (T.205). *Upper left*, .5"h x 5.0"w. Backstamp: 27.1. $60-90. *Upper right*, .38"h x 6.0"dia. Backstamp: 27.1. $30-60. *Lower left*, .88"h x 6.38"w. Backstamp: 27.0. $30-60. *Lower right*, .63"h x 6.0"dia. Backstamp: 27.0. $80-110.

Chapter V
Vases and Other Items Pertaining to Flowers

In this chapter there are photos of items which, in one way or another, pertain to the display of flowers or at least to the use of parts of them (e.g., in potpourris). They are clustered into the following categories:

This chapter is organized along the same lines as the others in this book. Thus, the basic categories (e.g., flower frogs, urns, wall pockets) are sequenced alphabetically. The vases group, which is by far the largest, has five named subgroups that also are ordered alphabetically. To facilitate the search for a particular vase, those subgroups are defined with reference to two features that anyone will notice instantly when looking at any vase. These are (1) the number of handles it has and (2) whether the vase is in a figural form or has a figural element. Within these subgroups, the vases generally are sequenced with reference to height. The main exception to this rule is that vases of similar shape but different size are sometimes clustered together. Because these groups and subgroups are defined in terms of simple, readily determined features, users of this book should be able to locate any vase of interest quite rapidly and easily. And that is the point.

Although vases (including wall pockets which, although a kind of vase, are placed in their own group) predominate in this chapter, some of the more attention-getting items are not vases. Consider, for example, the flower frogs shown in V.415 and V.416 or the hanging planter in V.417. Is there a more dramatic, eye-holding motif in this chapter than the one on the urn shown in V.421? I doubt it. Figural features are used regularly to add drama to Noritake items, and vases are no exception. The motif on the first such vase shown in this chapter, V.426, would be striking by itself but the addition of the large figural bird pushes it up a notch or two. The next vase, with eight figural birds, has long been a favorite with collectors and now, as was noted above in Chapter 2, we can date it with considerable precision. The Morimura Bros. ad in the *Crockery and Glass Journal* tells us that in December

1925, this blank was being shown as a new item ready for distribution in 1926.

Throughout this book, I have given preference, when I had the option, to photos that show groups of three or more similar items. I hope those looking at these photos will pause and appreciate the considerable effort (and fun) required in order for collectors to produce such groupings. Near the start of this chapter, the first such photograph (V.430) shows five fine figural bird vases. Midway in the chapter, photo V.487 shows 11 vases that are alike in shape and similar in beauty while V.489 shows six attractive post-war vases. Near the very end of the chapter, there are two photos showing multiple examples of the same wall pocket shape: V.546 with five items and V.547 with, count 'em, 14 (fourteen!) different small wall pockets with figural bees.

How tall is the tallest Noritake-era (1921-1931) vase? Only time and the efforts of many collectors will settle this one. In my first Noritake book, I noted (p.253) that the tallest vase I had ever measured was 12.75"h (although I did not have a photo of it) and so far that is still the tallest vase I have measured. In this book, two vases that size are shown (V.432 and V.498) but, as you will see when you look at them, they both have a *lot* more going for them than mere size. Many of the vases in this chapter have motifs that are unusual and/or exceptionally well conceived and executed—indeed far more than I can mention. I cannot resist at least listing the photo numbers of a few, however. I want especially to note the vases shown in V.458 because they are, in my opinion, two of the most elegant Deco Noritake vases that I know of anywhere (and, alas, they are not mine). I also would suggest that you take note of the motifs on the items shown in V.440, V.446, V.448, V.459, V.464, V.465 and V.466 (two fine examples involving the use of the Shinsha glaze), V.470 and V.471 (both being distinctive in part for the striking use of brown tones—uncommon colors for Noritake items from this era), V.499, V.501, V.503, V.540, V.518 (a rather unusual color) and V.519.

There are several photos in this chapter that show complete conceptual sets (for a discussion of such sets, see the Introduction to Part Two, above)—e. g., V.434, V.455, V.538 and V.540. But what I find even more interesting are certain of the *in*complete conceptual sets shown because they tell us of other items to look for. A terrific example is shown in V.444 and V.445 (taken together). Given what we see in those photos, it would seem all but certain that there must be a blue version of this motif on a vase like these out there somewhere but, I do not recall having seen one. The same can be said regarding the vases shown in V.456; is there one in green luster, or perhaps orange? The vases in V.478 are an interesting case. Keeping in mind the bowls shown in B.576, it seems that we can be fairly confident that a vase with a red version of the motif will be found. It also should be noted that the vases in V.478 are not alike in shape. Does this mean we can expect to find, eventually, oak leaf conceptual sets for *both* vase shapes? All collectors, we presume, will hope that the answer turns out to be "yes."

In the list of striking vase motifs given above, I excluded wall pockets and basket vases in order to give them their due separately. Two of the most striking and creative motifs shown in this book, let alone this chapter, are to be found on the basket vases shown in V.495 and V.496. And with conceptual sets in mind, consider the motif on the items in V.495 and V.515; is it not likely, in view of the motifs we see, that there is a third one featuring a background of blue checkerboard squares and a bold abstract floral? I certainly hope so! And finally, we turn to the section on wall pockets which, as in previous books, features some very impressive items. Although all deserve comment, I will merely direct your attention to several particularly outstanding and/or unusual items: V.531, V.532, V.536 (a new blank in my experience). The piece de resistance, however, is surely the item shown in V.545; it is both rare and superbly decorated. But these are only my thoughts on what is shown in this chapter; have a look for yourself and (as I am sure you will) come to your own conclusions as to what appeals to you.

Flower frog (V.415). 4.75"h x 5.25"w. Backstamp: 27.1. $250-350.

Ferner (V.413). 3.88"h x 8.0"w x 5.38"d. Backstamp: 27.1. $70-120.

Flower frog (V.416). 4.75"h x 5.25"w. Backstamp: 27.1. $250-350.

Ferner (V.414). 3.13"h x 4.88"w x 5.25"d. Backstamp: 27.0. $50-100.

Hanging planter (V.417). 5.0"h x 5.88"w. Backstamp: 27.1. $100-200.

Potpourri (V.418). 7.63"h x 5.38"w. Backstamp: 16.4. $100-150.

Urn (V.421). 8.5"h x 6.25"w. Backstamp: 19.1. $200-300.

Urn (V.422). 10.38"h x 5.0"w. Backstamp: 27.1. $110-180.

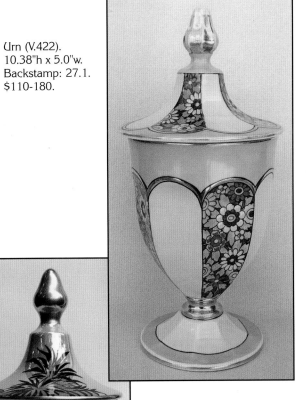

Potpourris (V.419). *Left*, 4.25"h x 4.75"w. Backstamp: 27.1. $90-140. *Right*, 4.25"h x 3.25"w. Backstamp: 27.0. $70-90.

Urn (V.420). 11.75"h x 5.75"w x 4.25"d. Backstamp: 19.1. $170-220.

Urn (V.423). 9.25"h x 4.25"w. Backstamp. 27.1. $140-210.

Urns (V.424). 9.38"h x 4.13"w. Backstamps: 27.0. Each, $90-120.

Vase (V.427) with figural elements. 7.0"h x 7.0"w. Backstamp: 27.1. $440-520.

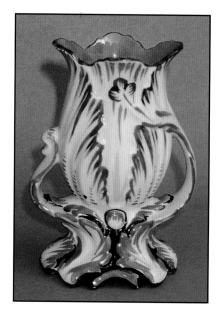

Vase (V.428) in figural form. 5.5"h x 4.25"w. Backstamp: 27.1. $90-180.

Urns (V.425). 9.38"h x 4.13"w. Backstamps: 27.0. Each, $100-140.

Vase (V.426) with figural element. 8.25"h x 5.0"w. Backstamp: 27.0. $150-200.

Vase (V.429) with figural elements. 5.5"h x 3.5"w. Backstamp: 27.1. $120-220.

Vases (V.430) with figural elements. 5.0"h x 4.0"w x 3.0"d. Backstamps: orange, 19.0; white, 26.0; gray-black 27.1; blue and tan, 27.0. Each, $100-200.

Vases (V.434) with no handles. 9.5"h x 4.0"w. Backstamps: 29.1 (29812). Each, $750-900.

Vase (V.431) with figural element. 5.13"h x 3.5"w x 3.25"d. Backstamp: 27. $130-220.

Vase (V.432) with no handles. 12.25"h x 5.75"w. Backstamp: 27.0. $140-240.

Detail (V.434A) of center vase (V.434).

Vases (V.433) with no handles. 10.75"h x 4.63"w. Backstamps: 65.019. Each, $30-70.

Detail (V.434B) of right vase (V.434). (A comparable detail of the vase on the left is shown in *Noritake Collectibles A to Z*, p.265.)

Vase (V.435) with no handles. 9.13"h x 3.75"w. Backstamp: 27.1. $150-200.

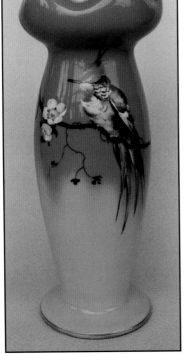

Vase (V.438) with no handles. 9.13"h x 3.25"w. Backstamp: 65.019. $40-80.

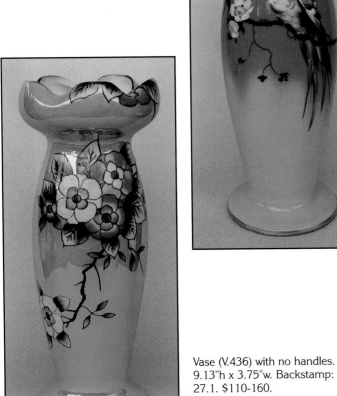

Vase (V.436) with no handles. 9.13"h x 3.75"w. Backstamp: 27.1. $110-160.

Vase (V.439) with no handles. 9.0"h x 3.0"w. Backstamp: 65.019. $40-80.

Vase (V.440) with no handles. 9.0"h x 4.75"w. Backstamp: 19.1. $190-290.

Vases (V.437) with no handles. 7.0"h x 3.25"w. Backstamps: 27.1. Each, $150-200.

Vase (V.441) with no handles. 8.63"h x 3.5"w. Backstamp: 67.019. $20-40.

Vases (V.442) with no handles. 8.63"h x 4.0"w. Backstamps: 19.1. Each, $40-80.

Vase (V.444) with no handles. 8.63"h x 2.88"w. Backstamp: 27.1. $140-190.

Vase (V.445) with no handles. 8.63"h x 2.88"w. Backstamp: 27.1. $140-190.

Vase (V.446) with no handles. 8.5"h x 5.38"w. Backstamp: 27.0. $140-190.

Vase (V.447) with no handles. 8.25"h x 3.75"w. Backstamp: 27.0. $40-90.

Vases (V.443) with no handles. 8.63"h x 4.0"w. Backstamps: 27.0. Each, $660-100.

Vases (V.448) with no handles. 8.13"h x 4.63"w. Backstamps: 27.0. Each, $100-150.

Vase (V.451) with no handles. 7.75"h x 5.25"w x 4.25"d. Backstamp: 27.0. $150-250.

Vase (V.449) with no handles. 8.0"h x 5.75"w. Backstamp: 27.0. $180-280.

Vase (V.452) with no handles. 7.75"h x 5.25"w x 4.25"d. Backstamp: 27.0. $100-200.

Reverse (V.452A) of V.452.

Vase (V.450) with no handles. 8.0"h x 4.5"w. Backstamp: 27.0. $90-170.

Vase (V.453) with no handles. 7.63"h x 3.5"w. Backstamp: 27.1. $100-180.

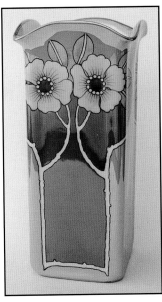

Vase (V.454) with no handles. 7.63"h x 3.5"w. Backstamp: 27.0. $120-200.

Vase (V.457) with no handles. 7.25"h x 3.63"w. Backstamp: 16.4. $80-120.

Reverse (V.457A) of V457.

Vases (V.455) with no handles. 7.5"h x 2.75"w. Backstamps: 27.0. Each, $100-150.

Vases (V.458) with no handles, arranged to show different features of the motif. 7.13"h x 4.63"w. Backstamps: 25.1. Each, $300+

Vases (V.456) with no handles. 7.5"h x 2.75"w. Backstamp: 27.0. Each, $60-90.

Vase (V.459) with no handles. 7.0"h x 5.38"w x 3.5"d. Backstamp: 27.1. $120-170.

Reverse (V.459A) of V.459.

Vases (V.460) with no handles. 7.0"h x 5.38"w x 3.5"d. Backstamp: 27.1. Each, $90-140.

Vases (V.463) with no handles. 6.75 "h x 3.0"w. Backstamps: 65.019. Each, $40-90.

Vase (V.461) with no handles. 6.88"h x 3.5"w. Backstamp: 27.0. $120-180.

Vase (V.464) with no handles. 6.63"h x 5.13"w x 3.25"d. Backstamp: 27.0. $100-200.

Reverse (V.464A) of V.464.

Vase (V.462) with no handles. The motif is one scene that encircles the vase. 6.75"h x 5.13"w. Backstamp: 27.1. $90-140.

Vase (V.465) with no handles. 6.63"h x 3.5"w. Backstamp: 55.5. $90-140.

Alternate view (V.462A) of V.462.

Vase (V.466) with no handles. 6.25"h x 3.88"w. Backstamp: 65.5. $80-120.

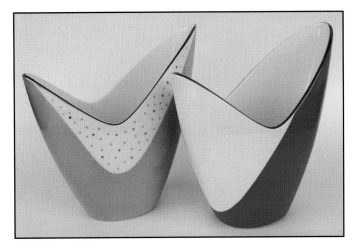

Vases (V.469) with no handles. 6.5"h x 6.63"w x 3.5"d. Backstamps: 77.3. Each, $40-90.

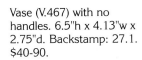

Vase (V.467) with no handles. 6.5"h x 4.13"w x 2.75"d. Backstamp: 27.1. $40-90.

Vase (V.470) with no handles. 6.38"h x 5.5"w. Backstamp: 27.1. $150-250.

Reverse (V.470A) of V.470.

Vase (V.468) with no handles. 6.5"h x 4.13"w x 2.75"d. Backstamp: 27.1. $40-90.

Vase (V.471) with no handles. 6.38"h x 3.38"w 2.13"d. Backstamp: 27.1. $90-160.

Alternate view (V.471A) of V.471.

Vases (V.472) with no handles. 6.38"h x 3.0".
Backstamp: 27.0. Each, $30-60.

Vase (V.475) with no handles. 6.25"h x 5.63"w.
Backstamp: 36.056. $40-90.

Vases (V.473) with no handles. 6.38"h x 3.0".
Backstamp: *Left,* 27.1; *right,* 27.0. Each, $40-70.

Vase (V.476) with no handles. 6.25"h x
5.0"w. Backstamp: 25.1. $40-90.

Vase (V.474) with no handles.
6.38"h x 3.0"w. Backstamp:
19.2. $60-100.

Vase (V.477) with no handles.
6.0"h x 4.0"w. Backstamp:
27.0. $50-100.

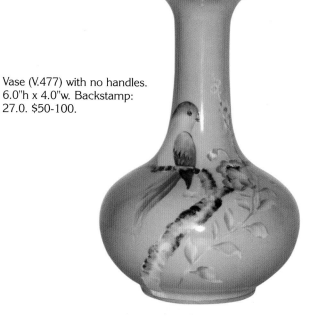

Vases (V.478) with no handles. *Left*, 5.88"h x 4.5"w x 4.5"d. *Right*, 6.0"h x 4.5"w x 3.63"d. Backstamps: 27.0. Each, $140-200.

Vases (V.481) with no handles. 5.88"h x 6.88"w. Backstamps: 27.1. Each, $80-120.

Vase (V.479) with no handles. 6.0"h x 3.5"w. Backstamp: 27.1. $60-100.

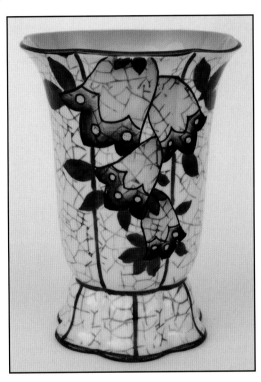

Vase (V.480) with no handles. 5.88"h x 6.75"w. Backstamp: 27.1. $180-240.

Vase (V.482) with no handles. 5.5"h x 4.25"w. Backstamp: 27.1. $40-90.

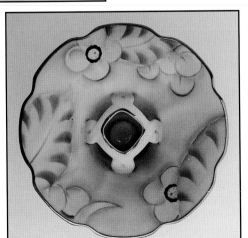

Alternate view (V.480A) of V.480.

Vases (V.483) with no handles. 4.63"h x 2.5"w. Backstamps: *Left*, 27.1; *others,* 27.0. Each, $30-50.

Vases (V.487) with no handles. 4.38"h x 2.13"w. Backstamps, *left to right*: 27.0, MIJ.0, MIJ.1, 27.1, 16.0, MIJ.0, 27.0, MIJ.0, 27.0, MIJ.0, 27.0. Each, $30-90.

Vases (V.484) with no handles. 4.5"h x 2.5"w. Backstamps: 47.056. Each, $20-40.

Vases (V.485) with no handles. 4.5"h x 2.5"w. Backstamps: *Left,* 27.0; *right,* 27.1. Each, $30-50.

Vase (V.488) with no handles. Vase, 4.25"h x 5.25"w. Backstamp: 27.1. Flower frog insert, 2.5"h x 3.5"w. Backstamp J.1. As shown, $150-220.

Vase (V.486) with no handles. 4.5"h x 5.25"w. Backstamp: 27.1. $40-70.

Vases (V.489) with no handles. 4.25"h x 2.5"w. Backstamp: 65.019. Each, $20-30.

Vases (V.490) with no handles. *Left*, 3.0"h x 1.63"w. *Right*, 3.0"h x 1.25"w. Backstamps: *Left*, 40.3; *right*, 41.3. Each, $20-30.

Vases (V.491) with no handles. 3.0"h x 2.38"w. Backstamps: 64.019. Each, $20-30.

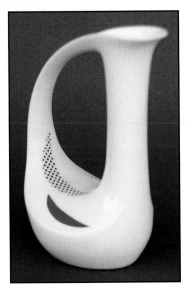

Vase (V.492) with one handle. 3.75"h x 2.75"w. Backstamp: 65.019. $20-30.

Basket vase (V.493). 10.0"h x 8.13"w x 6.13"d. Backstamp: 27.0. $100-150.

Basket vase (V.494). 10.0"h x 6.25"w x 4.0"d. Backstamp: 27.1. $300-400.

Basket vase (V.495).
7.5"h x 6.25"w x
4.75"d. Backstamp:
27.1. $250-350.

Basket vases (V.497). 7.5"h x 6.13"w. Backstamps: 27.0. Each, $80-130.

Reverse (V.495A)
of V.495.

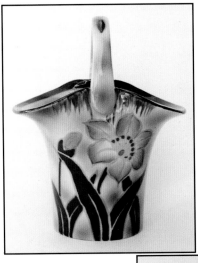

Basket vase (V.496).
7.5"h x 6.25"w x
4.75"d. Backstamp:
27.1. $250-350.

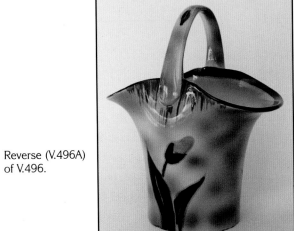

Reverse (V.496A)
of V.496.

Vase (V.498) with two handles. 12.75"h x 9.0"w x 6.5"d.
Backstamp: 18.0. $300-450.

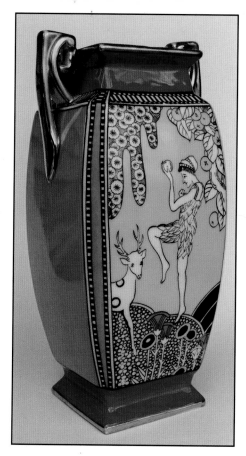

Vase (V.499) with two handles. 9.75"h x 4.5"w. Backstamp: 27.0. $500-600.

Vase (V.500) with two handles. 9.75"h x 6.13"w x 3.13"d. Backstamp: 27.0. $250-350.

Reverse (V.500A) of V.500.

Reverse (V.499A) of V.499.

Vase (V.501) with two handles. 10.38"h x 5.63"w x 5.25"d. Backstamp: 19.0. $220-320.

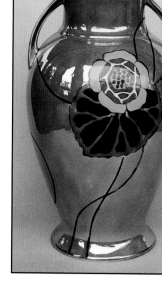

Vase (V.505) with two handles. 9.0"h x 5.0"w. Backstamp: 27.0. $250-350.

Vase (V.502) with two handles. 10.63"h x 7.63"w. Backstamp: 27.0. $250-350.

Alternate view (V.502A) of V.502.

Alternate view (V.505A) of V.505.

Vase (V.503) with two handles. 10.0"h x 6.75"w x 6.25"d. Backstamp: 27.0. $250-350.

Alternate view (V.503A) of V.503.

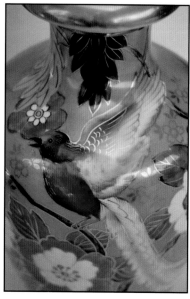

Vase (V.506) with two handles. 8.88"h x 6.75"w. Backstamp: 19.1. $50-100.

Vase (V.504) with two handles. 9.75"h x 5.25"w x 5.0"d. Backstamp: 27.0. $250-350.

Detail (V.504A) of another example of the vase in V.504.

Vase (V.507) with two handles. 8.88"h x 6.75"w. Backstamp: 19.1. $50-100.

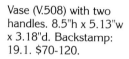

Vase (V.508) with two handles. 8.5"h x 5.13"w x 3.18"d. Backstamp: 19.1. $70-120.

Vase (V.510) with two handles. 6.88"h x 6.0"d. Backstamp: 27.0. $80-120.

Pair of vases (V.511) with two handles. 6.5"h x 4.75"w. Backstamps: 19.1. Each, $60-90.

Vase (V.509) with two handles. 8.5"h x 5.38"w x 3.25"d. Backstamp: 19.1. $60-110.

Vases (V.512) with two handles. 7.0"h x 4.0"w. Backstamps: 27.0. Each, $60-90.

Vases (V.513) with two handles. 6.0"h x 4.88"w x 3.63"d. Backstamps: 27.0. Each, $90-140.

Vases (V.514) with two handles. 6.0"h x 4.88"w x 3.63"d. Backstamps: 27.0. Each, $80-120.

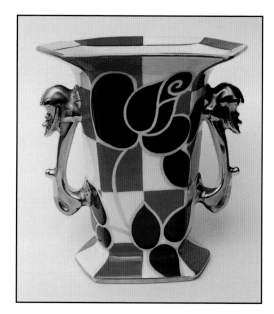

Vase (V.515) with two handles. 6.25"h x 5.5"w x 4.38"d. Backstamp: 27.1. $200-250.

Reverse (V.515A) of V.515

Vase (V.516) with two handles. 6.25"h x 6.0"w x 4.63"d. Backstamp: 27.1. $150-200.

Vase (V.517) with two handles. 6.0"h x 3.75"w. Backstamp: 27.0. $50-100.

Vase (V.520) with two handles. 7.5"h x 5.25"w x 4.25"d. Backstamp: 27.0. $50-100.

Vase (V.518) with two handles. 5.75"h x 3.75"w x 3.5"d. Backstamp: 27.0. $50-100.

Reverse (V.520A) of V.520.

Vase (V.519) with two handles. 5.25"h x 7.63"w x 2.25"d. Backstamp: 27.1. $200-300.

Vase (V.521) with two handles. 6.5"h x 4.75"w x 2.5"d. Backstamp: 31.7. $40-90.

Vase (V.522) with two handles. 5.5"h x 3.88"w. Backstamp: 27.0. $350-500.

Vase (V.525) with two handles. 6.0"h x 5.38"w x 1.88"d. Backstamp: 27.1. $70-110.

Reverse (V.525A) of V.525.

Vase (V.526) with two handles. 5.0"h x 3.75"w. Backstamp: 27.0. $120-190.

Pair of vases (V.523) with two handles. 5.5"h x 3.75"w. Backstamps: 27.0. Each, $120-170.

Vases (V.524) with two handles. 5.5"h x 3.75"w. Backstamps: 27.0. Each, $50-100.

Vases (V.527) with two handles. 3.13"h x 2.25"w x 2.0"d. Backstamps: *Center*, 16.4; *others*, 27.0. Each, $30-50.

Vases (V.528) with two handles. 2.25"h x 2.0"w. Backstamps: *Left,* 16.0; *right,* 16.4. $20-30.

Wall pocket (V.530). 11.88"h x 3.88"w. Backstamp: 27.0. $400-600.

Detail (V.530A) of V.530.

Vase (V.529) with three handles. 5.88"h x 3.75"w x 3.63"d. Backstamp: 27.0. $110-180.

Wall pocket (V.531). 8.5"h x 3.88"d x 3.0"d. Backstamp: 27.0. $550-750.

Wall pocket (V.532). 8.5"h x 3.5"w.
Backstamp: 27.0. $350-550.

Wall pocket (V.535).
9.25"h x 4.88"w x
2.63"d. Backstamp:
27.0. $300-500.

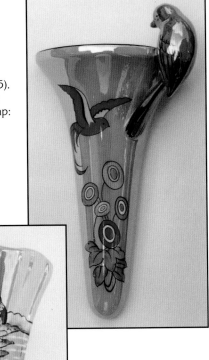

Wall pocket (V.533).
9.25"h x 4.38"w.
Backstamp: 27.1.
$120-180.

Wall pocket (V.536).
8.13"h x 4.75"w x 2.5"d.
Backstamp: 19.1. $100-
150.

Wall pocket (V.537).
8.0"h x 4.63"w x 2.63"d.
Backstamp: 27.1. $90-
180.

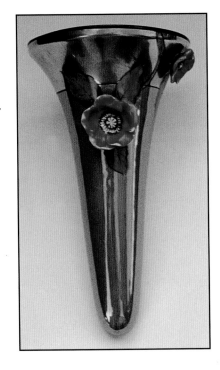

Wall pocket (V.534). 9.5"h x
4.75"w. Backstamp: 27.0.
$300-500.

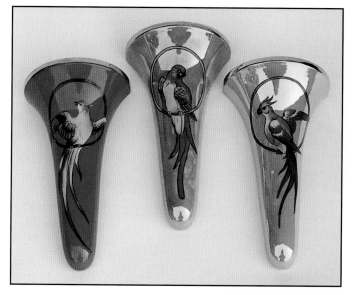

Wall pockets (V.538). 8.0"h x 4.63"w x 2.63"d. Backstamps: 27.0. Each, $90-180.

Wall pockets (V.541). 6.63"h x 5.0"w. Backstamps: 27.0. Each, $230-330.

Wall pocket (V.539). 8.0"h x 4.63"w x 2.63"d. Backstamp: 27.1. $150-230.

Wall pockets (V.540). 8.25"h x 2.38"w. Backstamps: 27.1. Each, $80-130.

Wall pocket (V.542). 8.0"h x 3.88"w. Backstamp: 19.0. $280-380.

Alternate view (V.542A) of V.542.

Wall pocket (V.543).
7.13"h x 4.25"w.
Backstamp: 27.1.
$150-200.

Wall pockets (V.546). 7.0"h x 3.25"w x 1.75"d. Backstamps: 27.1.
Each, $70-120.

Wall pocket (V.544). 5.5"h x 7.75"w. Backstamp: 27.0. $300-500.

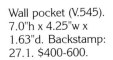

Wall pocket (V.545).
7.0"h x 4.25"w x
1.63"d. Backstamp:
27.1. $400-600.

Wall pockets (V.547). 5.0"h x "2.13"w x 1.38"d. Backstamps: 27.0,
for all except the gray pocket; it is 27.1. Each, $120-220.

Miscellaneous Items

This chapter contains photos of the following miscellaneous collectible Noritake fancyware items:

Advertising items (p.218)
Bells (p.218)
Biscuit (or cracker) jar (p.218)
Celery freshener and serving set (p.219)
Coaster (p.219)
Egg warmer (p.219)
Juicer (reamer) (p.219)
Kitchen match holder (p.219)
Napkin rings (p.219)
Painting on porcelain (p.220)
Place card holders (p.220)
Shaving mug (p.220)
Spooners (p.220-221)
Toast racks (p.221)
Tooth pick holders (p.221)

One of the goals I had while selecting the materials shown in this book was to get as many photos into it as I can. One of my aims in selecting the materials for this chapter, on the other hand, has been to put as few into it as I can. Moreover, I must not do this simply by reducing the number of photos but, instead, by working to keep to a minimum the number of things that *must* be shown in it—i.e., things that can not reasonably be included in one of the other chapters.

The array of items in this Chapter Z is somewhat broader than in the three previous Z Chapters. A particularly interesting new addition is advertising items. Many collectors like to be able to add to their displays a small and nicely crafted sign that says "Noritake." Examples of some post-war signs are shown in Z.66 and Z.67. A few collectors have room for the giant platters, plates and cups and saucers that were used in store displays to attract customers. An example of this type of advertising material is shown in Z.68. There are many other kinds of Noritake display signs. Some especially rare and interesting ones are shown in Morikawa's *Masterpieces of Early Noritake* (see *Bibliography*).

Throughout the book, although not in every chapter, I have made various comments about Noritake "conceptual sets." The classic example is a set of three items that have the same motif or three closely related ones and three luster colors (tan, blue and green). The bells shown in Z.69 represent two-thirds of such a set, with the missing item being a tan bell. As it happens, just such a bell was the first item shown (Z.1) in the first Chapter Z (in *Noritake Collectibles A to Z*). Someday, it would be fun to photograph all three of them when they are in the same place at the same time.

One of the more unusual and important items shown in the photos of this chapter can be seen in Z.72. In my *Collectible Noritake A to Z*, I showed an orange version of the largest item in Chapter V on the assumption that the item was a vase. When I photographed it, I did think it was a little odd that somebody would have decided that *celery* should be on a flower vase and, indeed, I said as much (see p.170 of *Collecting Noritake A to Z*). Not long after the book hit the streets, a collector friend told me she had such a "vase" as well as the 6 individual salt cups that went with this "celery freshener and server." The set you see in Z.72 is *that* set. As is probably obvious by now, the user of this set is supposed to put freshly cut celery stalks in the vase-like server so that the stalks can absorb cold water which will help to make or keep them crisp. At meal or snack time, the server can be brought from the refrigerator and placed on the table along with an invitation to "help yourself."

One could suggest, I suppose, that such a serving set is a "special purpose bowl" and should thus be shown in Chapter B. But really; do you think someone with an interest in that sort of item would think to look for it in the chapter on bowls and boxes? I don't think so. And for the same reason, I did not think there were adequate grounds for putting it in Chapter P with "multi-piece serving sets" (which this thing is). Although there are salts with this set, I could not see that this made it suitable for Chapter C (condiment items) either. Finally, I also felt there were no good grounds for putting it in Chapter V; I did that once and was (with reason) laughed out of court. So for good or ill, here we are, in Chapter Z. Amidst all this uncertainty, there is one thing that is certain: the celery freshener and server set shown in Z.72 is a *terrific* item. Moreover, knowing of this green set and the orange celery "vase" shown in V.245, "conceptual set theory" would suggest strongly that there should be a blue set out there someplace. Knowing how beautiful blue non-luster Noritake items can be, I hope someone finds it soon. I'd love to see it.

Several more items call for at least a few brief comments. Is the round flat thing shown in Z.73 really a coaster? I am not sure. With such an elaborate motif, I am dubious. It could be an ashtray, I suppose, but...well, without rehearsing all that was said above about the celery serving set, I finally decided to put it here and call it what most collectors call it—a coaster. *Noritake* reamers of the sort shown in Z.75 were not at all common during the core of the so-called Noritake era of 1921-1931; the backstamp on the item in Z.75 suggests it is a rather early piece (perhaps as far back as 1908-1910). Kitchen match holders that are as fresh looking and bright as the one shown in Z.76 are seen very infrequently.

The exquisite painting on porcelain shown in Z.78 is a recent piece, probably less than 20 years old. Given that one theme of this volume is the century of creative work by the Noritake Company, it seemed more than appropriate to me that it should be included. The backstamp on it is used primarily on items intended for the domestic market. The ceramic material this painting is on is about 1/4 inch thick. Given the term being used for this piece, it perhaps should be noted that it has been fired.

Curiously enough, the items referred to routinely by collectors as "spooners" are often the subject of considerable debate: are they really for spoons? For some of these items (e.g., those shown in Z.81-Z.84) there seems to be general agreement that they are meant to hold tea spoons, even though they don't do so in exactly the same way. But what about the item shown in Z.85? Is it a spooner? Doubters have noted that it is too short to hold spoons and so they insist (usually) that it is a "candy dish." I tend to reply by saying that almost every Noritake fancyware bowl can be thought of as a "candy dish" and so I avoid the phrase like the plague. In short, I simply do not know *the* answer. One thing I do believe, however, is that most Noritake collectors *call* these things "spooners" (whether they are or not) and so they will look for them here with the rest of the (real?) spooners. So, for now, I

consider the case closed. If, on the other hand, you have solid evidence that establishes what the function of the item shown in Z.85 is/was, please let me know (via Schiffer Publishing).

Bells (Z.69). 3.75"h x 3.0"w. Backstamps: 27.1 Each, $90-140.

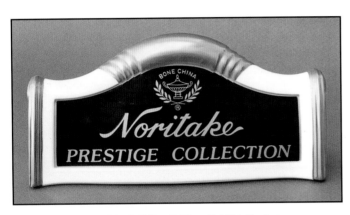

Advertising item (Z.66). 3.25"h x 7.5"w x 2.13"d. Backstamp: none. $30-60.

Advertising item (Z.67). 1.38"h x 5.88"w x 1.13"d. Backstamp: J.5. $30-60.

Biscuit (or cracker) jar (Z.70) with silver handle and lid. 8.38"h x 6.0"w. Backstamp: 16.4. $110-150.

Advertising item (Z.68). Cup, 5.13"h x 11.13"w x 9.25"d. Saucer, 1.5"h x 14"dia. Backstamp: 74.5. $130-180.

Biscuit (or cracker) jar (Z.71). 5.33"h x 8.0"w x 5.25"d. Backstamp: 27.1. $40-80.

Celery freshener and serving set (Z.72). Vase, 6.63"h x 6.5"w x 4.13"d. Backstamp: 27.1. Individual salts, 1.5"h x 2.25"w. Backstamps: MIJ.1. Set, as shown, $170-220.

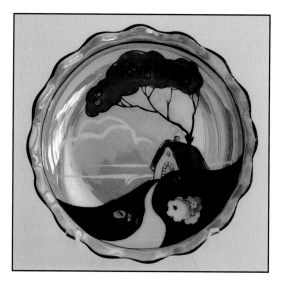

Coaster (Z.73). .63"h x 4.25"dia. Backstamp: 27.1. $20-40.

Egg warmer (Z.74). 3.63"h x 5.63"dia. Backstamp: 27.0. With matching porcelain stopper, $90-140.

Juicer (or reamer) (Z.75). 3.38"h x 4.5"w x 4.25"d. Backstamp: 16.4. $40-90.

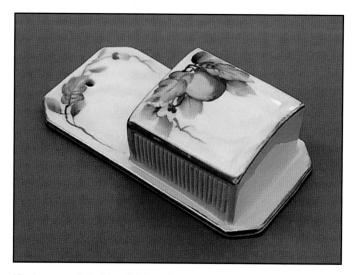

Kitchen match holder (Z.76). 4.38"h x 2.25"w x 1.13"d. Backstamp: 27.0. $40-90.

Napkin rings (Z.77). 2.63"h x 2.25"w. Backstamps: 27.0. Each, $20-40.

Painting on porcelain (Z.78). 8.88"h x 6.13"w. Backstamp: 76.7. $100-200.

Detail (Z.78A) of Z.78.

Place card holders (Z.79). 1.5"h x 1.38"w. Backstamps: 27.1. Set of 6, $90-120.

Shaving mug (Z.80). 3.75"h x 4.75"w x 3.88"dia. Backstamp: 27.0. $70-100.

Top view (Z.80A) of Z.80.

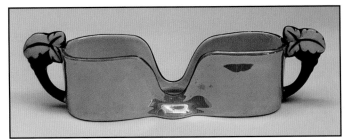

Spooner (Z.81). 2.38"h x 8.75"w x 2.0"d. Backstamp: 27.1. $30-60.

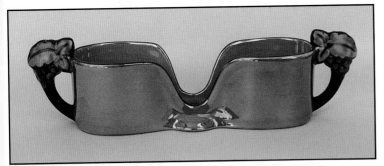

Spooner (Z.82). 2.38"h x 8.75"w x 2.0"d. Backstamp: 27.1. $30-60.

Double spooner (Z.85). 2.13"h x 6.38"w x 3.75"d. Backstamp: 27.0. $30-60.

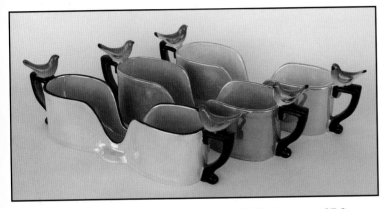

Spooners (Z.83). 2.75"h x 8.25"w x 2.0"d. Backstamps: 27.0. Each, $40-70.

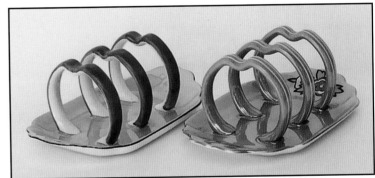

Toast racks (Z.86). 2.0"h x 5.63"w x 3.75"d. Backstamps: 27.1. Each, $50-90.

Double spooner (Z.84). 2.75"h x 4.88"w x 3.25"d. Backstamp: 27.0. $30-60.

Toothpick holders (Z.87). 2.0"h x 2.75"w. Backstamps: *Left,* 27.1; *right,* MIJ.1. Each, $30-60.

Bibliography

Altounian, Rachel. 1998. "U.S. Exportation of Nippon Porcelain." p.10 of Van Patten 1998 (see below).

Altounian, Rachel. 1998. "The Morimura Porcelain Factory." p.11 of Van Patten 1998 (see below).

Altounian, Rachel. 1998. "Baron Ichizaemon Morimura." p.12 of Van Patten 1998 (see below).

Anon. "Morimura Bros. Celebrate." *Pottery, Glass and Brass Salesman*, Vol. XXXIV, No.16, November 18, 1926, pp.9-11. New York: O'Gorman Publishing Co.

Anon. "Baron Morimura Dies in Japan." *Crockery and Glass Journal*, Vol. 90, No.12, September 11, 1919, pp.9-11. New York: Demarest Publications, Inc.

Aoi, Kohtaro and Kazuhiko Kimura. 2001. *Old Okura China, Toyotoki and Nagoya Seito: Japanese Modern Tableware, 1910s-1940s*. Osaka, Japan: Tombow Publishing Co., Ltd.

Benton, Charlotte, Tim Benton and Ghislaine Wood, eds. 2003. *Art Deco 1910-1939*. Bulfinch Press, AOL Time Warner Book Group, Boston, New York and London.

Brewer, Robin. 1999. *Noritake Dinnerware: Identification Made Easy*. Atglen, PA: Schiffer Publishing, Ltd.

Coddington, Barbara, Stanford Sivitz Shaman and Patricia Grieve Watkinson. 1982. *Noritake Art Deco Porcelains: Collection of Howard Kottler*. Pullman, WA: Museum of Art, Washington State University.

Donahue, Lou Ann. 1979. *Noritake Collectibles*. Des Moines, IA: Wallace-Homestead Book Company.

Ercoli, Giuliano. 1989. *Art Deco Prints*. Linda Fairbairn, trans. New York: Rizzoli.

Fukunaga, Ikuo. 2001. "The Morimura Brothers Connection." pp.44-47 in Van Patten 2001 (see below).

Hida, Toyojiro. 1996. *Early Noritake*. Nagoya, Japan: The Noritake Company, publisher.

Kimura, Kazuhiko and Kohtaro Aoi. 1999. *Noritake China 1891-1945: Collector's Guide*. Osaka, Japan: Tombow Publishing Co., Ltd.

Kimura, Kazuhiko and Kohtaro Aoi. 2001. *Noritake's Art Deco and Bone China*. Osaka, Japan: Tombow Publishing Co., Ltd.

Levie, Alison, trans. 1998. *French Art Deco Fashions in Pochoir Prints from the 1920s*. Atglen, PA: Schiffer Publishing, Ltd.

Morikawa, Takahiro. 2003. *Masterpieces of Early Noritake*. Kyoto, Japan. Maria Shobo Co., Ltd., publisher.

Murphy, Pat. 2001. *Noritake for Europe*. Atglen, PA: Schiffer Publishing, Ltd.

Nakashima, Tomoko. 2000. "The Vogue for Things Japanese in the American Aesthetic Movement" Volume 4, *The Komaba Journal of Area Studies* (Tokyo), pp.157-175.

Noritake Company, The. 1997. *Noritake: History of the Materials Development and Chronology of the Backstamps*. Authored anonymously and published by the Noritake Company, Nagoya, Japan.

Ohga, Yumiko. 1998. Old Noritake in Japanese Art. Tokyo, Japan. Corona Books, publisher.

Ohga, Yumiko and Tsuneko Wakabayashi. 2001. Masterpieces of Nippon Porcelain. Tokyo, Japan. Heibonsha Co., Ltd., publisher.

Ohga, Yumiko. 2002. Old Noritake in Japanese Art. Tokyo, Japan. Heibonsha Co., Ltd., publisher.

Spain, David H. 1997. *Noritake Collectibles, A to Z: A Pictorial Record and Guide to Values*. Atglen, PA: Schiffer Publishing, Ltd.

Spain, David H. 1999. *Collecting Noritake A to Z: Art Deco and More*. Atglen, PA: Schiffer Publishing, Ltd.

Spain, David H. 2002. *Noritake Fancyware A to Z: A Pictorial Record and Guide to Values*. Atglen, PA: Schiffer Publishing, Ltd.

Suzuki, Keishi. 2001. "About Old Noritake." pp.5-12 of the separately published English translation of the Japanese text in *Masterpieces of Old Noritake*, Yumiko Ogha and Tsuneko Wakabayashi, editors; Aki Oga Kato and Judith Boyd, translators. Tokyo: Heibonsha Publishers, Ltd.

Tailor, Heather. 1990. *Lustre for China Painters and Potters*. London, B.T. Batsford, Ltd.

Vandervoort, Diana. 1992. *Temari: How to Make Japanese Thread Balls*. Tokyo, Japan: Japan Publications Trading Co.

Van Patten, Joan F. 1979. *The Collector's Encyclopedia of Nippon Porcelain*. Paducah, KY: Collector Books.

Van Patten, Joan F. 1982. *The Collector's Encyclopedia of Nippon Porcelain, Second Series*. Paducah, KY: Collector Books.

Van Patten, Joan F. 1986. *The Collector's Encyclopedia of Nippon Porcelain, Third Series*. Paducah, KY: Collector Books.

Van Patten, Joan F. 1997. *The Collector's Encyclopedia of Nippon Porcelain, Fourth Series*. Paducah, KY: Collector Books.

Van Patten, Joan F. 1998. *The Collector's Encyclopedia of Nippon Porcelain, Fifth Series*. Paducah, KY: Collector Books.

Van Patten, Joan F. 2000. *The Collector's Encyclopedia of Nippon Porcelain, Sixth Series*. Paducah, KY: Collector Books.

Index